Contents

Introduction and overview

This book is intended to help with AS level standard project work in Information and Communications Technology (ICT). It does not contain a whole sample project or seek to say 'this is exactly what you have to do', but gives guidance on how to approach project work, and provides ideas for techniques to use.

For many people ICT projects at this level will be the hardest piece of project work they have ever attempted, and also the biggest in terms of volume and complexity. As with all problems, projects become more manageable if broken down into smaller parts. This book is arranged with this in mind.

You will find that there is more advice included on the earlier parts of the project; this is because it is in the early stages that most things start to go wrong. Time and care spent early on makes the later parts of the project work much easier.

In all of the work that you do, it is important to remember just what ICT is about. It is simply the use of technology to input, store, process, transfer and output information. So every project must be concerned with these things. Different businesses and individuals do these tasks in different ways but everything comes down to these five stages, no matter how complex it seems to begin with.

So why do you have to do project work?

The answer is simple: to test your ability to apply the knowledge that you have gained through theory work in a real or realistic situation. It also allows you to learn skills and techniques that cannot be taught through theory work alone.

When your project work is assessed the marker is not just looking at your skill with one or more software packages, but in your ability to provide an ICT solution to a problem – something that involves a whole range of skills. This is why projects are assessed over a range of criteria and categories from analysis to evaluation.

Planning out your work, keeping to deadlines set and organising yourself are important life skills; all of these are needed to complete the project successfully. More marks are probably lost through not completing sections, for example design work, than through an inability to do the work.

What does project work involve?

For AS level your project work is based on producing a solution to a **task-related problem** that is **limited in scope** and is for a **real or realistic** end user. It may be that your teacher actually sets a task or choice of tasks for you to do, or you may be expected to find a real end user yourself. The important thing is that you will learn to specify and devise a solution, implement the solution (build it), document the solution, test the solution does what it is supposed to do and evaluate the success of the solution. You are encouraged to develop your solution as you learn more about the software that you are using and improve the solution when testing shows up errors, so that the whole process is one of continual development.

All project work in ICT attempts to encourage you to adopt what has become in many cases 'best practice' in the industry. Over the years many problems have been caused by solutions that have simply been created by programmers to do what they **think** the end user wants. Often this was not what the end user actually did want and so the business failed to benefit.

Also many solutions have been badly documented. This leads to tremendous problems when a program needs updating, a member of staff leaves or something needs to be added to the program. Lack of documentation and forward planning led to many companies spending large sums of money trying to cure problems with the year 2000 date change, or adjusting programs to cope with the euro.

Project work should be a challenge. It should be fun. It should keep you interested and busy. You will get a feeling of satisfaction from providing a solution to someone's problem that does what it is supposed to do. It will not always go smoothly: you will have problems, you will get fed up and frustrated, but this can happen when you do anything challenging. You will learn a lot, not just in terms of ICT but also about solving problems, communicating with people, being self critical (very important in ICT), helping others and producing a detailed piece of work to a high standard that you can be proud of. Many students use their project work when going for jobs, or as the basis of work needed for higher level courses. So enjoy and learn.

2

Choosing a task for your AS project

Perhaps the first problem that you will have is in finding an idea to base your project on. The AQA ICT3 specification states:

> **'For this project candidates will be expected to tackle a task-related problem which will have limited scope and will be a self contained problem.'**

When you first start to study ICT at AS level you may or may not have not done GCSE ICT. Just because you haven't studied GCSE does not put you at a disadvantage, apart from possibly with the level of knowledge of software that you have. (This is something that you can pick up with practice fairly quickly.) What is important is to recognise what the subject of ICT is concerned with and why anyone should ever want to use ICT – something that is often taken for granted.

Why does anyone use ICT?

When you study the theory parts of the course you will learn that there are certain things that ICT is good at. Among other things, it can:

- offer an improved speed of processing data or a more accurate result
- be used continuously and be more reliable than a human
- improve presentation
- improve speed and standard of communications
- provide new opportunities for businesses

It is important that you realise just what ICT can do for a business/organisation, and the advantages and disadvantages of using it. Companies do not invest large amounts of money in ICT systems without getting a benefit back to the business.

Remember too that all types of organisation can be used – they do not need to be private/public companies, but can also be charities, voluntary or state organisations, societies and private clubs.

So the sorts of situation where ICT is used are where there is:

- boring repetitive work
- mistakes/lack of accuracy
- poor presentation
- lack of security
- poor organisation of data
- lack of time
- shortage of money
- lack of information for decision making

A task-related problem

The points above should get you thinking about the types of problem that might make good projects – but what about the element of realism? Experience shows that a problem that is real will provide you with far more scope to gain good marks on project work than one that is made up. The worst thing that you can do is to invent a problem or try to produce a solution for yourself. The problems if you do this are, firstly, you may **think** that you know what is needed when in fact you don't, and secondly, you will find that you are not motivated to succeed in the same way as when you produce a solution to a problem for someone else.

How to find a project?

Projects can cover many different types of task for:

- small or large businesses
- clubs and societies

- home/leisure
- schools
- charities and voluntary organisations
- family or friends
- neighbours
- past and present teachers
- your own part-time jobs

Some students pick up project ideas when they are doing work experience with companies, or use a contact made in the past with a company to get ideas.

Small businesses are often very keen to get help, for example painters and decorators, builders, plumbers, gardeners, hairdressers, physiotherapists, farmers, market gardeners, cake makers, dressmakers, upholsterers, or small garages. Most self-employed people or those acting as consultants rarely have time to sort out their business administration: they are too busy actually doing the work and earning money. Usually they are quite willing to let students do projects for them: they might get a good workable solution if you do a good job, and if not, all they will have lost is some time.

Large organisations should not be ignored. Individual departments or members of staff may often want a solution to a specific problem that is causing them trouble.

Sometimes students try to pick a problem that is totally unrealistic or where there is already a perfectly suitable ICT solution available. Areas to avoid include:

Payroll usually too complex, with tax tables, etc.
Stock control difficult in large organisations, or where there is a need for very rapid turnover, or where automated data entry would be essential, or where goods are bought in different units to the ones they are used/sold in (this is possible but needs care).

Some ideas are:

- invoicing or quotation systems for small businesses
- websites for any organisation, club, society, hotels, caravan parks

- ordering systems
- payment recording
- timetabling/booking for freelance trainers, aerobics teachers, part-time staff, delivery staff, church halls, sports facilities
- sports events, scheduling classes, recording results
- publicity material for organisations/presentations
- appointment schedules
- analysis of statistical/financial data
- record keeping of different sorts e.g. for animal breeders, collections, hiring out equipment

These are just a few very general ideas that could be looked at, but should give you a starting point. It is important that you find a contact you feel that you can talk to and ask questions. If you do something for your parents or a relative, be sure that they will be prepared to help and won't always be away on business, or be too demanding!

Remember it is possible to take a task for which there is already an ICT solution but where the solution has become outdated, or doesn't do everything it is needed to do.

Warning

You must of course be careful not to pick a problem that is too large or complex, and this is where your teacher will be able to help. However, you must help them advise you by being able to describe your idea well enough for them to be able to say 'Yes, this is suitable' or 'No, this is not suitable because…'.

Choosing software

You may find that your teacher will have decided what type of software you are going to use to produce your solution, or you may have been given a free choice. If they have already chosen the type of software this will be because they feel that you can achieve the best projects using a particular piece of software. If you are given a choice, make sure that you discuss the options carefully with your teacher. Don't choose something that no one at school/college can help you with. You may think that you know enough about the software, but in order to get good marks you will need to use what are described as 'advanced features' and for these you will probably need some help!

Your teacher also needs to be able to state that what you produce is all your own work, so you will need to be able to demonstrate what you produce and work on it in school. This means that if you are going to be working at home, or elsewhere, you must be careful not to use a version of your chosen software that is incompatible with your school's version. Also you will need to make sure that you have a way of 'transporting' your work from school to home – this may sound easy, but be careful about file sizes, especially if you are using anything with graphics in it!

Some final advice on project choice: you should choose something that you are going to be interested in, or that is a challenge to you, or that you will enjoy working on. It is too big a piece of work to be uninterested in, as you will get bored and then won't feel like putting in that extra effort needed to get a good grade. Do not forget that the project work for AQA AS ICT is worth 40% of the marks for the AS; exam papers are only worth 30% each. It is very unusual for students to get a good grade if their project work is weak, but it is possible to use your project work to help boost your marks if you aren't very good at exams.

TO DO

Read up on what sort of problems ICT is good at solving.

Start asking around for project ideas.

Discuss possible choices of software with your teacher, as this will influence the sort of task you look for.

Make sure you know what sorts of problem are suitable for solving with the software that you are going to use.

Describing your selected task

An outline and problem statement

One of the most important things that will affect the quality of your project work is that you make a sensible choice of project that is realistic for you to do. Some students are better with more of a challenge, whilst others can gain higher marks by doing all of the sections well and not feeling as if they have taken on too much.

This is where it is important that you describe clearly for your teacher what you are intending to do. Don't say 'I'm doing something for my uncle's garage', or 'for my neighbour's shop'. This would be no help at all: your uncle could work for a branch of a major car dealership and your neighbour could manage a branch of a major supermarket. In these cases they would potentially not be suitable problems, as the operation might be too big or too complex. In business, problems that might sound simple can require a very complex solution – one example of this is timetabling.

It is also important that anyone reading your project must be able to tell easily what it is about, right from the first page. Most important of all, **you** need to be able to understand what you are trying to do!

A sample outline and problem statement for a business:

Springer Landscapes

Springer Landscapes is a small landscape gardening business run by Finn Raffles. He started the business five years ago when he was made redundant, and has slowly built it up so that now he employs two men to help him with the labouring.

Finn does all of the paperwork for the business himself, with the help of his wife. He finds this time consuming, boring and difficult at times, as he often makes mistakes in calculations and can end up losing money on jobs. Finn says 'This is the worst bit of this job, I wanted to work outside and now I'm spending too much time in the office.' Most of Finn's business comes by word of mouth or as a result of the small advert he has in the local paper. He says that if he could get the paperwork sorted out then he could take on more staff and expand, as there 'seems to be plenty of business out there'.

Finn has about 50 customers for whom he does regular work, such as lawn mowing, pond maintenance and hedge trimming. He also does one-off jobs for other customers. These could be anything from clearing an overgrown garden to laying a path or building walls, rockeries or patios, and so on. It is these jobs that cause most paperwork.

For these jobs Finn is usually contacted by telephone and arranges to visit the customer to discuss the job. Before the visit he will record in his diary:

- the date and time of the appointment
- the customer's name, address and telephone number(s)
- what is needed, e.g. a wall, patio, fence

When Finn gets to the customer he records further details about the job such as:

- measurements
- type of materials required, bricks, stone, wood, etc.
- date needed by/convenient dates

Finn records some of these details in his diary – he uses a big page-a-day diary and will also draw sketches and make notes on a spiral notepad that he keeps in the van.

When he next gets time he will calculate the time needed to complete the work (for example, he knows it takes about one day to build six feet of stone wall with two men working), the cost of materials needed for the job and the cost of labour. He then has to add on something for his profit and to cover overheads like running his van, tools and equipment, and office costs. He then prepares an estimate, handwritten on a piece of headed paper, which his wife will then photocopy and send out with a standard letter stating terms and conditions – for example, the estimate is valid for 14 days.

Finn tries to keep details of his estimate: these are photocopies kept in a box file. He sometimes loses these or takes a long time to find them when a customer telephones, which makes it difficult to keep track of jobs, materials and costs.

Eventually, after a week or even a month, a customer may decide to have the work done and get back to Finn. Finn then books the job into his diary.

Finn has a computer at home in his office which his wife uses for preparing letters, and which is used by his children for homework and games. He himself is not very familiar with computers, although he is thinking of buying a digital camera so that he can use it for pleasure, and to take photos of jobs to remind him when he is preparing estimates.

As can be seen, Finn has several problems that could possibly be solved by the use of ICT. His biggest problem is preparing the estimates, as this is something he needs to do himself, and if he gets it wrong it can have a big effect on his business. If the estimate is too high he can miss out on work; if it is too low then he can lose money on the job; if he loses a copy of an estimate he looks unprofessional.

The task I am going to provide a solution for is:

Finn's biggest business problem: the time it takes to work out accurately, record and make copies of estimates and file these so he can easily find them again when needed.

As you can see the description includes information about the business:

- what it does
- the size of the business (number of employees and number of customers)
- what sort of information the business uses (estimates, letters, diary)
- who does what (Finn gets details from customers, calculates estimates, his wife sends letters)
- the problems the business is having (paperwork time consuming, inaccurate, gets lost, business can't expand, etc.)
- the main task that the student intends to solve

You will notice that the student has said that they are going to tackle one particular problem – that of preparing and storing estimates. Don't just say 'I am going to computerise Springer Landscapes'. This shows little understanding or appreciation of what is involved in a business and is not a suitable task – it is far too general and you would only end up with a very simple solution that didn't look at a problem **in depth**.

Willington Rangers

Willington Rangers is a football club that was formed nearly fifty years ago. It is based in the city of Maningham and has its own ground and small clubhouse. The area in which it is based has a very 'mobile' population: people who live there tend to be young families, couples and single people who often leave the area for new jobs or to buy bigger houses.

There are six teams: two under tens, two juniors and two seniors. The football club usually has about 200 members, some of whom are supporters rather than playing members. Willington Rangers belongs to the North West league and all the teams play matches once a week on a Sunday morning during the season. These may be at home or away. They also have one regular practice session a week on Tuesdays for the under tens, on Wednesdays for the seniors and on Thursdays for the juniors.

Some of the matches can be a long way away as the club is on the outskirts of the city, and other teams in the league come from both the city and the surrounding countryside.

A committee of volunteers runs the club. The only employee is a groundsman and general caretaker. The committee is made up of the Chairman, Treasurer, Secretary, Social Secretary and three other members who act as the team managers for each age group. They are elected on an annual basis and give their time for free.

The club gets income from the subscriptions paid annually, fundraising, hiring the ground out to other clubs and a small grant from the Sports Council. Members who attend training sessions and team members pay a small fee for each training session or match to cover the immediate costs, such as getting a referee.

The main problems facing the club are a decrease in the number of members and the difficulty of communicating with team members about matches. The committee would like to raise the profile of the club by making its existence known to new people coming in to the area. They are also wondering whether they can find a cost-effective way of communicating with members, as bills for telephone calls, photocopying and postage can be quite high. For example, if details of each away match have to be given to all team members, then that means about 80 copies have to be produced (as the club does not provide transport, members have to make their own way to matches).

Results from matches played are published in the local paper that comes out on a Thursday evening. Unless they attended a match or training session members don't know how the teams got on until then. The committee think that the under tens find it encouraging to see how the senior teams are doing.

The club is wondering about setting up a website that could be used as a method of advertising and communicating with members and prospective members, and that could improve the reputation of the club and help to get sponsors or people who want to rent the facilities. Some of the things that they have thought of which could be put on a website are:

- history of the club and past successes
- map of location
- details of membership – possibly a membership application form to print off
- details of training sessions
- results of this season's matches
- detailed write-ups and results from the last games played
- teams selected for next matches
- details of away games, maps, times, etc.
- links to other relevant sites so people can find the Willington Rovers site; ideas are:
  - the local council
  - estate agents
  - football association
  - sporting suppliers
  - other teams in the league

The task that I am going to provide a solution for is:

To produce a website that the secretary of the club can use to advertise the club and communicate with members, prospective members and the wider public, football and business communities.

This is a very different type of problem to the one for Springer Landscapes, but you can see that the content of the outline is similar:

- what the organisation does
- the size of the organisation (number of members and number of teams)
- what sort of information the organisation uses (team lists, maps, match results, application forms)
- the problems the organisation is having (volunteers giving up time, reduction in membership, costs of contacting people and passing on information, etc.)
- the main task that the student intends to solve

There is not a lot of information in the description to indicate who does what at the club, and the student is going to need to find this out before they can start. For example, who has the information on the history? Who deals with membership applications? Who arranges the teams and match venues? Who will have all the results information?

TO DO

Think about who would be the best person at Willington Rovers for the student to talk to to find out the answers to the above questions. Who is going to be the end user of the solution? Is there going to be just one end user?

It is impossible to tell you exactly what you need in the description of your organisation/problem area, as all projects are different, but you should be able to see the sort of questions that you need to be able to answer. Remember that ICT is concerned with the way in which we collect, process, store, transfer and communicate information, so that is what you are looking at in your projects.

Once you know the task for which you will provide a solution, you know what your **aim** is. An aim is an overall target for your project work. Some examples would be:

'to create an automated invoicing system for Fred's builders'

'to produce a website for XYZ company that will allow them to advertise their services to a wider audience'.

How do you find out about your chosen organisation/ business or task?

It is important to remember that, with any project, you are looking at how data is converted into information. The data is your input, the processes are the conversion and the information is your output. This is what ICT is all about, and this is common to all projects. This is also what makes collecting sample documents important, as these are one way in which data is moved around. Can you think of other ways of moving data? This should help you to think about exactly what you need to find out about.

Ideas for techniques to use

Interviews

The most popular method of finding out information for your **requirements specification** is to conduct an interview with the proposed end user. This is not, however, the easiest thing to do. Here are some points to consider if you are going to conduct an interview.

1. Always prepare for an interview. Can you find out any information about the business in advance?
2. Who is the end user? Is there just one person or are there several? Will they all want to do the same things?
3. How are you going to arrange the interview? Will you write a letter to ask them to see you and arrange a date and time? This can be useful as you can send in advance a copy of the questions that you want to ask, to give people time to consider them beforehand.

The other advantage of doing this in advance is that it may save time for your end user. You have to remember that they are doing you a favour by spending time with you.

4 A copy of any letter sent (and, even better, the reply received) can be put into your project. If you use emails to set up or conduct a meeting then include copies of these.

5 Always be polite, and explain why you need the person's help and how important it is for your exam work. Remember 40% of your AS level marks are on the project – even (or especially!) parents need reminding of this.

6 What questions are you going to ask? You must plan these out beforehand. Look at the sample descriptions in Chapter 3 and think about what you would need to ask to gain that information.

7 Don't have too many questions. You will probably only need to ask about ten. Any more and you will be taking up too much time and also get too much information at once.

8 Think about how you are going to record the answers to your questions. Having the questions on one piece of paper and putting the answers on another can be difficult if you are sitting on a chair and trying to juggle everything around. It is better to use just one piece of paper and leave spaces to put the answers in.

9 Another idea is to use a Dictaphone or tape recording device of some type. If you can get one of these it will be useful, as it is often hard to remember everything that has been said, or write it down, and manage to concentrate at the same time. If you use a recording device, ask permission from the person you are interviewing first.

10 Always write up the results of an interview straight away afterwards, before you forget what the notes you made meant.

11 It is useful, and polite, to send a copy of your write-up of the interview to the interviewee and ask them to sign it as a true record of the interview. This has several advantages – you can get confirmation that what you have written is correct, it gives you the chance to include any questions that you forgot to ask or now realise you need the answers to, and it gives you more evidence to go in your project. You also know that you are working with correct facts

rather than your interpretation of what was said.

12 Ask whether you can have copies of any documents used by the business, such as invoices, quotes, membership application forms, appointment cards, customer records, and so on. These could be blank or preferably contain data.

Other ways of finding out about the business

1 **Research** There are plenty of sources that you can use to get information about a company. Things like advertising material, company accounts and reports, company newsletters, and advertisements in papers or websites can all help you to understand what the business is involved with. If they are a charity or a club then there may be newsletters, membership details and publicity material. Even small businesses usually advertise somewhere. Bigger companies may even have written procedures or guidelines for doing things.

2 **Observation** This is probably one of the most useful and most neglected skills. Asking to watch a clerk producing orders or invoices, a receptionist making appointments, a builder preparing quotations are all invaluable. Often when people explain what they do they miss things out. An example would be:

> 'When I prepare an invoice I put in the customer's code, I get details of what they want and put the prices in for each item and then work out the VAT, any discount and the total amount.'

In this description the end user has said nothing about where they get the customer code or customer address details from. There is nothing about where the prices come from and how the calculations are done, and what the discounts are.

If you had observed the person preparing the invoice you would have seen where they got the customer details from, and the prices, and so on. The other advantage is that you are not asking the person to stop working and talk to you, so businesses may be happier to let you do this than take up time. You can always arrange an interview later to ask about things you have seen. Whatever you do, you will have a far better idea of what goes on.

3 Looking at similar organisations   If a business is new or wants something that they haven't already got, then what about studying a similar business to see how they do it? For example, if your task is to produce a website, visit similar company websites and look at what is good and bad about them from the point of view of a visitor to the site; also ask your end user what they like or don't like about them. If you are producing a leaflet/advert/menu then collect other ones and discuss which style/layout/colours and fonts your end user likes. If it is a presentation you are making, then have you seen others, and what made them more or less effective?

4 Studying documentation   Sometimes you may have a task to look at that is already partly or fully automated using ICT but has become inefficient or outdated. In this case you need to actually study any documentation, designs or printouts from the current system to help you to work out what it is doing. **But** don't just rely on what is there. If someone wants something replacing or improving it means that there are things wrong with it, so you still need to find out exactly what the processes are that it is automating – otherwise you just end up with another ineffective solution.

TO DO

- Write a description for an idea that you have come up with. You will need to do some investigation first, but this might just be having an informal chat with a neighbour/employer or parent.

- Get your teacher to look at your idea so that they can decide whether it is suitable for you to attempt, and whether it is suitable for solving with the software that you are going to use.

- You will need to word process most of your project report. Start by creating a folder to put all the work for your project in.

- Think about how and when you are going to 'back up' your work at school and at home. You are an ICT student so exam boards don't accept excuses for having 'lost' your project due to the computer 'crashing', the dog eating your disk, and so on!

- Get an envelope folder or something similar to store all of the work that is on paper. Keep rough notes, copies of any emails to end users, any copies of documents that you pick up from the organisation, and so on. This will make it less likely that you will lose things, and also makes it easier to take work between home, school and end user.

Describing your task in detail

Now you have agreed the task that you are going to use for your project work, it is worth looking at the criteria you must meet in order to gain the best marks on the **requirements specification**.

For good marks, the criterion in the AQA specification for AS ICT states:

> 'A *detailed* requirements specification has been produced for the identified *problem*, which *matches the needs* of the stated *end-user(s)*.'

I have highlighted the most important words in this criterion so that you can see that the specification must be *detailed*; the *problem* and *end user* must be clearly stated; and the solution that you design must *match the end user's needs*. The following section describes how to gather the detail.

Describing your task in detail

Once your idea is approved by your teacher, you will need to describe the task in detail. You may need to break it down into smaller sub-tasks. For instance, if you are going to produce an advertising leaflet you may need to define exactly the different bits making up the leaflet (a logo, headings, address details, map, pictures and so on) and also more detailed information about who the leaflet is being targeted at, or who will be responsible for producing it. For a website you will again have to find out similar details about the content and intended visitors.

Here are some typical questions that you will have to answer if you are considering word processing/desktop publishing/presentation-type tasks:

- Just who is your end user for this system?
- How is the information proposed for your product distributed to people at present?
- What methods of reproduction are used?
- How many copies are produced at any one time?
- How frequently are copies needed?
- How often does data change?
- How much does it cost to produce copies now?
- What are the problems with how the material is produced now?
- Is the material currently produced in house or by an external agency?
- What benefits are likely from changing the system?
- What style does the company wish to portray? – This is where you could show your end user examples of the sorts of style available. You could use anything from other similar leaflets to book covers, to find out what styles your end user likes.
- What paper size and quality is used now?
- Is a logo needed – how is it available?

Fixed and Variable Data

For a good desktop publishing/word processing project, whatever you pro-duce should preferably not be a one-off; it should be reusable. For this to be the case you should produce a template containing all **fixed data** that is to appear every time the letter/invoice/leaflet/ticket/badge is produced, and all of the settings required for font size, and so on.

The data that is changed on the separate occasions the leaflet is produced is known as the **variable data** – it changes each time you produce a new version.

As part of your specification you must discover what data is to be fixed, and what is variable.

- Typical examples of fixed data could be company name and address,

maps, logos, lists of telephone numbers, extensions, fax numbers, opening hours and so on.

- Variable data might be the letter content, special offers, prices, items for sale, photographs, articles and so on, depending on your application. It is the variable data that will be your test data later – so make sure you have got examples of it.

You can always include annotated sample documents to show the sort of data you have got to deal with.

Production criteria

Don't forget to find out whether borders are required and where white space should be included, whether there are tear-off portions or places where a fold line must go.

Remember that you will also by now have constraints such as the printable area and quality/orientation of paper that you must work within.

Remember that for word processing projects you need to be including conditional mail merges and so will have different paragraphs being inserted in different letters. This is the sort of thing that gives advanced functionality and also makes testing easier. Don't be tempted to use templates already available.

You should now have an idea of the tasks that you are going to need to complete. Only when you have established what is needed can you proceed to design.

Processes and task descriptions

The key thing for ICT3 projects is to ensure that you clearly state what the **inputs, processes** and **outputs** required are.

Remember:

- The end user of a website is the person you produce it for, **not** the visitors to the site.

- The end user of a leaflet is the person you produce it for, **not** the people who look at it.
- The end user of a presentation is the person you produce it for, **not** the viewers of the presentation.

If you are producing a solution that is going to be solved using database management software or spreadsheet software then you will need to find out the exact way the processes are carried out now – how is an invoice prepared? How does a customer make an appointment?

Below is an example of a description of someone preparing an invoice; this was produced after observing the person at work.

1 Orders are received by telephone (the clerk fills in a blank order form) or by post, and orders are filed in '**orders awaiting invoices' file** in date order.

2 *Pick* the next order form from the '**orders awaiting invoices' file**.

3 Get **blank invoice** form from pile in filing cabinet.

4 Get **customer file**.

5 *Check* customer on order has a customer number; if not, *allocate one* using file.

6 *Copy* customer details on to blank invoice.

7 *Get* **catalogue** of products.

8 *Read* first item ordered on order form.

9 *Look up* description of item from code number.

10 *Fill in* code number and description.

11 *Look up* quantity ordered on order sheet.

12 *Enter* on to invoice.

13 *Look up* unit price using code and quantity.

14 *Calculate* price (unit price × quantity) and enter on to invoice.

15 *Repeat* stages **8** to **14** until no products left on order form.

16 *Calculate* total and enter.

17 *Calculate* value added tax (VAT) and enter.

18 *Calculate* net price and enter.

19 *Get* **invoice summary sheet**.

20 *Get* next invoice number from summary sheet (last number plus 1).

21 *Enter* invoice number on invoice.

22 *Enter* dates on invoice.

23 *Copy* details on to invoice reply slip.

24 *Copy* invoice details on to invoice summary sheet.

25 *File* invoice using invoice number in **unpaid invoices file**.

26 *File* invoice summary sheet.

What does this description tell us?

All words in *italics* are verbs or 'doing words'; they involve an action or process.

All items in **bold** are stores of data or 'files' of some description.

So it starts to give an idea of what our solution has got to involve – what the software must do and what is needed in the way of data to do it. We know that the output is the invoice itself, and also the invoice summary sheet.

Another way of doing this

Some people find it difficult to write such a detailed description and prefer to draw a diagram to illustrate what is happening. Your teacher will

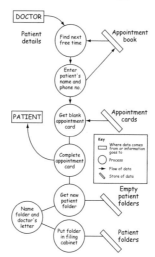

Figure 5.1 shows an example of a diagram to show the task of a medical specialist's secretary making an appointment with the specialist for a patient referred by a doctor.

probably have a preferred way of doing this, so listen to them.

The diagram is just a rough hand-drawn one. It uses some symbols to illustrate certain items that need to be shown:

- where data comes from or information goes to
- the movement of data
- the processes involved
- any data stores that are used in carrying out the task

What is missing?

We now have a reasonable idea of what the basic inputs, processes and outputs are, but neither the description nor the diagram gives us any idea of exactly what the customer details are, or what a product description looks like, or what details are recorded about the patient or appointment.

How can we get this?

The easiest way to find out the details we need about inputs and outputs is to get hold of copies of them. In the examples above this would mean getting hold of a completed invoice, the customer file and the catalogue of products, or the appointment card, patient folder, and appointment book – all sample documents that should be collected when you investigate the business.

Obviously in some case it is impossible to bring the sample documents away with you, but perhaps you can take a photocopy of a page of an appointment book, or a sheet out of a catalogue.

Be careful that you substitute imaginary names for real ones – you do not want to reveal private and/or confidential data!

Sample documents and what they can provide

Figures 5.2–5.5 show you examples of some sample documents of the sort that you might collect. They also show what you can find out from them and the sort of questions that they should make you start to ask your end

HILL HOUSE LIVERY STABLES

LIVERY AGREEMENT

Client details

Name of Client: ....

Address: ....

....

Telephone Number: ....

Horse details

Name of horse/pony: ....

Sex: .... Colour: ....

Age: .... Height: ....

Any allergies/special conditions we should know about: ....

....

....

....

Feed: AM: .... PM: ....

....

....

....

....

Shows details about the client, the horse and the contract between the client and livery owner.

Client details

Name of veterinary surgeon: ....

Telephone number: ....

Name of farrier: ....

Telephone number: ....

Insurance company: ....

All of the details are INPUTS.

Type of livery: ....

Monthly rate: ....

Terms: ....

....

....

....

Contract details

Liveries are accepted on the following terms and conditions. Prior to taking up occupancy these terms shall be accepted by the client by signature.

TERMS AND CONDITIONS

1   All fees are payable monthy in advance. Extras, i.e. warmers, lessons, clipping, etc. will be billed in arrears.

Figure 5.2 Any type of agreement, membership form etc gives you the inputs that you need about clients or members. A completed agreement would give you more information. It would show what *format* the data takes, e.g. 'Name of Client' could be: Jane Smith, J Smith, Miss J.R. Smith, and so on.

HILL HOUSE LIVERY STABLES

LIVERY AGREEMENT

Name of Client: .... ROSE JONES ....

Address: .... 3 CARTER CLOSE, ...

.... KINGSDOWN ....

Telephone Number: .... 03254 763590 ....

Name of horse/pony: .... GILBERT ....

Sex: .... Gelding .... Colour: .... Bay ....

Age: .... 9 .... Height: .... 15.2 hh ....

Any allergies/special conditions we should know about: ....

.... Allergic to hay ....

....

....

Feed: AM: .... PM: ....

.... ~~hay (the ssoop)~~ ....

.... ~~or~~ Sports Mix .... Same as AM ....

.... 2 scoops ....

....

....

Name of veterinary surgeon: .... R. M. Hazlehurst ....

Telephone number: .... 07982 536748 ....

Name of farrier: .... Bert Black ....

Telephone number: .... 02345 769738 ....

Insurance company: .... ~~Wilbisfam~~ .... NFU ....

Type of livery: .... Full ? ....

Monthly rate: ....

Terms: ....

....

....

....

Liveries are accepted on the following terms and conditions. Prior to taking up occupancy these terms shall be accepted by the client by signature.

TERMS AND CONDITIONS

1   All fees are payable monthy in advance. Extras, i.e. warmers, lessons, clipping, etc. will be billed in arrears.

Figure 5.3 Here is a completed agreement which now shows the type and size of the data that is collected. Note changes to data made simply by crossing out old data.

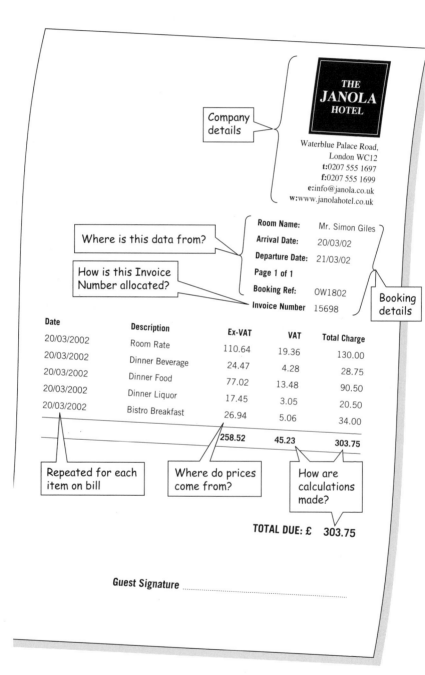

Figure 5.4 Sample document – annotated hotel bill.

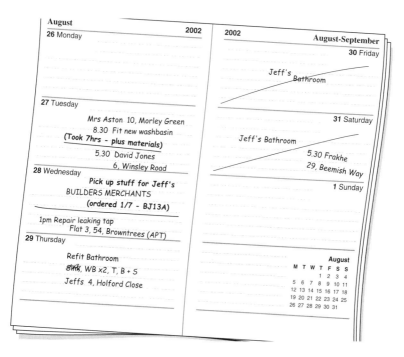

Figure 5.5 Sample document – pages from a plumber's diary.

user. This is why I find them really useful because I can talk to end users about them and ask questions such as:

- Where does this name and address come from?
- How do you know which invoice number to use next?
- Where do you keep a record of prices?
- What do these abbreviations in your diary mean?
- Do you like the format of this invoice?
- Is there anything else that you would like to include on the application form?
- How many items do you usually have on an invoice?

The list of questions can then be used to send to your end user, to email to them, to discuss with them, whatever is the easiest for you, but it means you are finding out what they want and how the task is carried out now. The chances are there will be lots of things that come out that they forgot to tell you about to begin with!

Inputs, processes and outputs

You should now have a good idea of the inputs, processes and outputs of the task for which you are going to provide an ICT solution.

It is very important that you be able to identify exactly what your solution needs to do (**processes**), what data is needed to do it (**input**) and what it is supposed to produce (**output**). Anyone marking your work will be looking to see whether you have **clearly** stated these. If you don't know what they are then you cannot produce a solution that actually does what it is supposed to do!

The criterion from the AQA AS ICT specification says:

> 'The input, processing and output needs, which *match* the requirements specification, are *clearly* stated.'

So if you miss out doing this you will find it difficult to get good marks. You also won't know what it is you are supposed to be doing!

How you write down your inputs, processes and outputs is up to you, but it is sensible to have a side heading in your project that clearly indicates where to find them. Remember that you do need to describe them in detail; it is not sufficient to say that a map or customer's details are the input, or a report is the output. You need to know exactly what is needed in them. Here are some examples of some poor descriptions and some better descriptions of inputs, processes or outputs:

Poor description	Better description
INPUT: Customer details	Customer first name
	Customer surname
	Name or number of house
	Street
	Town
	Postcode
	Telephone number (home)
	Telephone number (mobile)

Poor description	Better description
OUTPUT: Report of videos overdue	Header of name of store, and date and time report produced Sorted by number of days overdue, descending, subheadings for number of days Page numbers (if multi-page) as footer Including customer surname, customer number, video code, and video title in tabular format
OUTPUT: Page one of leaflet to contain a map of location of hotel	Map must contain hotel marked clearly with arrow All motorways and main A roads within 20 miles Nearest railway station – shown with red circle Nearest airport should be listed underneath with approximate time by car from hotel Places of interest in the region – using numbered symbols to include zoo, aircraft museum, adventure park
PROCESS: Calculate total cost of bill	Get sum of cost of all items Calculate VAT at current rate Display VAT Add VAT to sum of cost of all items Display total with VAT = amount owing Copy amount owing to next free line on invoice summary sheet

TO DO

Having looked at the sample documents in Figures 2 to 5, could you produce even better descriptions of the inputs, processes and outputs shown above?

What else do I need to find out about?

There is no point in coming up with a wonderful solution if the end user can't use it. To make sure that it can be used it is important that you consider what resources the end user has available.

Software available

You may need to consider not just the type of software the end user has, but the version of it, in case you need to save your solution in a different version for them to use. Remember to include not just the basic software such as word-processing, relational database management software, and so on, but also photo editing, scanning, draw/paint, browser software, and so on, and the operating system that is used. In many cases the software will not impose any constraints on what you develop, but it should be considered and you need to show that you have done so.

If the business does not currently own the software that you are going to be using, then investigate the cost for them and see if you can justify the cost on the basis of time or staff savings or increased business.

Don't include justifications for using one type of generic software rather than another if there isn't really an alternative. Perhaps consider instead one spreadsheet package compared with another, or different versions.

Hardware available

This is often a very poorly considered factor in project work. For many generic software packages the processor and memory capabilities of modern PCS is not an issue, although large relational database solutions may be slower on some machines with a lower specification.

You must, however, consider things such as:

- Printers – print quality, printable area (full bleed or not), types (weights) and orientation of paper that can be used, colour, cost of cartridges/other consumables
- Other peripherals available – do they have a CD drive or a CD re-writer (CD/RW), a tape streamer, a digital camera, scanner, speakers, LCD projector, plotters, etc?
- What is the screen they use like? – size, quality.

Remember: do not fall into the trap of simply listing what is available without making comments about what that actually means in terms of the solution that you can produce.

End user(s) skills

Many projects seem to be for novice users, but just what is a novice user? Is it someone who has never used a computer before? Or someone who hasn't used the particular generic package before? Is it someone who might only use the solution once a year or once a month, so is an infrequent user, or is it someone who will use your solution every day? Do you have just one end user or several with different skill levels? How old are your end users? Does this have an effect? The solution does not have to be for a novice; producing solutions for experienced users can actually be just as demanding on user interface design – if not more.

It is important that you give a clear idea of the skill level of the user(s), as the interface and user guide must be suited to their needs – that is why things like the age of the user can be important. There is a lot about interfaces to be covered in the theory modules, so use your knowledge gained from the theory to help you here.

Security

There may be a particular need for security to be incorporated into your solution. You need to find out whether the users need to be restricted or whether the data being used is sensitive. If this is the case you will have to ensure that the test data that you use is suitable – perhaps ask the company to provide some.

Data Protection requirements

Do not use real customer records or patient details in your project testing. You need to consider the requirements of the Data Protection Act. Would you be covered if you did use live data? Past projects have included sensitive data about people that is private. Even your parents may be unhappy if they discover their bank statements/bills/investments/payslips have been included without removing their names!

Cost

Sometimes it may be appropriate to consider the cost of solutions in your project. This is particularly the case where leaflets/publicity/promotional material is involved, where the main reason for justifying the solution may be the reduction in costs.

What do end users want?

Now that you have all the information that you need about the business, the problem and the task that you are to solve, you must look at what the end user actually requires from the solution. Many commercial products have failed in the past because the developers failed to do this. This is where having a real end user can help. If you try to make up requirements they are never quite right, and if you don't bother to find out your end user's needs then you won't know what you are trying to do!

End user requirements

Throughout your project you are concentrating on producing a computerised solution to a **business problem**. What the end user wants the system to do is the **business requirements**, and these are likely to be much more general and phrased in a way that describes what benefits the end user wants to see to the business or organisation. Examples might be:

> **'I want a system that will cut down the time my secretary spends on maintaining our customer file.'**
>
> **'I would like to be able to guarantee that all invoices are accurate and so avoid complaints from customers or loss of income.'**
>
> **'My clerk doesn't have any time to spend learning how to use a new system, and I can't afford to send her on a course as staff turnover is too high, so whatever we have must be simple.'**
>
> **'I need to be able to get more members for the club.'**
>
> **'I need to cut down on postage and duplicating costs.'**

The end user's requirements may be something that you can get them to write for you themselves, or else they must at least sign what you have written, to give their approval and confirm that this is what they want from the system.

You may need to help the user to specify their requirements – often asking them what is wrong with how things work now is useful. For example you might ask, 'Do you have any problems with customer records getting lost?' or 'Would it be useful to be able to sort customers into areas?' or 'Would it be helpful to see how long it takes a customer to take up a quote?' These questions can be prepared in advance and either used at an interview, sent by post, faxed or emailed. It is important that you include these.

From these requirements you then have to decide just what your solution is going to do and what you are trying to achieve. There are several ways of doing this and laying out your work, and your teacher will help decide on what is appropriate for you. Here are some ideas of the sort of thing that they may suggest, with some examples.

Objectives

Basically these set down what **you** want your system to do. They are much more specific than your aim and can help you to break down your solution into individual 'bits' that you can then work on. Some people do not include objectives but go straight on to devising **performance criteria** that are measurable and can be tested (see below).

Examples of objectives might be:

Objective 1: To reduce the input time for new customer details by 50%.

Objective 2: To achieve 100% accuracy in the calculation of invoices.

Objective 3: To produce a system that is easy for a beginner to use.

Objective 4: To produce a system that is capable of storing 100 customer records.

The first two of these are what are known as 'quantitative' objectives, as they can be tested by measuring. The fourth objective is also quantitative but will not be as easy for you to test – you would need to do calculations on record sizes, file sizes and disk space.

The third objective is 'qualitative' – a subjective assessment only can be made.

It is advisable to make as many of your objectives quantitative as possible. Achievement of the qualitative ones is generally only assessable by your end user. Note: most objectives can be made quantitative, even the last ones!

| Performance indicators or criteria

These are a different way of stating your objectives. They state the same thing, but by describing the intended results. Instead of saying 'I want my system to …', they are phrased 'The system should …'.

The four objectives above could be rewritten as performance criteria as follows:

1   The system should allow new customer details to be input in a maximum of 2 minutes (currently takes 4 minutes manually).
2   Invoice calculations should be performed to 100% accuracy.
3   A beginner should be able to use the system, once trained, without reference to the producer of the system.
4   The system should be capable of handling up to a maximum of 100 customer records.

Getting performance criteria right is fundamental to the success of the project. They help to determine your test strategy and plan.

In summary:

End user requirements are what the end user wants the solution to do for the business.

Objectives are what the solution needs to do to achieve the end user requirements.

Performance criteria are how you measure the success of the solution in meeting the end user requirements.

A little time spent on sorting out these things early on can ensure that you know what you are doing and will help to keep your project on track – many projects fail simply because the student doesn't really know what they are trying to do!

Testing becomes much easier to design and evaluation marks improve if you have a clear idea of what you are trying to achieve with the solution you are producing. Performance criteria help design testing and prevent the production of pages of repetitive testing that simply shows, for example, that buttons work!

Now you are ready to design your solution!

What is design and why is it necessary?

Designs are needed to see how someone has decided to solve a problem. They are necessary in business so that if the functions the solution is to provide change over time, or an error is found, someone (often not the original designer) can look at the designs and see exactly how the solution works. From this they can decide on amendments that are needed.

For your project work the marker needs to see that you understand how to produce designs and the need for them.

Design work will be different for different solutions based on different generic software packages. But no matter what you are producing at the end, your designs should be detailed enough for someone else with the same level of knowledge of the software to be able to produce a solution identical to yours.

You may find that it is impossible to produce an accurate design before you start implementing your solution. For AS level projects this is not crucial so long as you do make sure at the end that the designs you include in your project report meet the criteria set by the examination board.

Common errors in design work

- lack of detail – a third person couldn't reproduce what you have done
- failure to correct designs when changes have been made while the solution is being developed

- poor presentation of designs – a third person couldn't read or understand the design work, often because it is too scruffy, too small or contains too much detail on one sheet of paper
- lack of designs for processes
- too much concentration on input screen designs
- inefficient designs – often indicate lack of appreciation of the software
- pages and pages of design work that could be covered using far less paper
- lack of accurate designs for output, e.g. reports, letters
- testing designs are superficial and/or incomplete, strategies and test data aren't included
- testing design does not test that the solution does what it is supposed to do (meet the performance criteria)
- designs are actually implementation

What do I need designs for?

You need designs for:

1. User interface, including error messages where these can be customised, and user guides/help
2. Inputs
3. Processes
4. Outputs
5. Testing, including end user testing
6. Overall flow/structure of the solution
7. Any procedures that have to be followed to use the solution, e.g. installation, back up, security

Exactly what is needed depends on the generic software package on which your project is based. The next chapters give some ideas on design work for different generic software.

Before or during your design work you should make a list of all of the elements of the solution. This could be a list of all the worksheets, macros and user forms you need for a spreadsheet solution; or a list of tables, forms, queries, reports and macros for a database solution.

Making a list will help you to keep track of what you need to produce designs for. It will also give you some idea of how much work you have to do – so it should help you to plan your time!

What you are trying to achieve

The AQA AS ICT criteria state that for work in the highest mark band of the requirements specification

> **'Effective designs have been completed which would enable an independent third party to implement the solution'.**

This means that someone else can pick up your design work and complete the solution in **exactly** the same way that you will do. The next sections describe how to make sure your designs can be used by someone else.

The overview

No matter what software you are designing your solution in, a diagram that illustrates an overview of the solution will help you and the person marking your project to find their way around it. This is important no matter how simple or complex the task. If you don't feel you have enough material to bother doing one, then the chances are your task is too simple for a project!

Often the easiest way to show an overview of your solution is by using a diagram. It doesn't matter what this is like, so long as if you use symbols you include a **key** – this is true of any diagram you produce.

Figure 7.1 shows a very rough overview diagram for a solution to a task of producing invoices that is to be designed using spreadsheet software. The same sort of diagram can be produced for any solution, regardless of what software you are using. It could be made more complex by using different

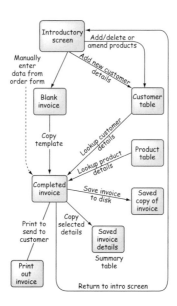

Figure 7.1 Simple overview of a design for a solution to the task of producing an invoice.

symbols for paper output, output to disk, user forms or worksheets, but ask yourself: does it need to be any more complex, or does it do its job adequately already?

The next sections give advice on design for projects based on different types of software, but here are some general guidance points to remember:

- To produce an effective solution that is useable by the end user in the end user's environment, it is essential that for all but the most technical end users the solution be easy to use. Don't expect your end user to add data in the datasheet level directly into the data source using a relational database management system. Don't expect them to be able to type directly into a text frame in desktop publishing projects. Make it easy for them!
- You will probably find that the solution you produce will change as you develop it from the initial design. This does not matter: it shows that you are learning more about the software or about the user's problems, or that the user has changed their mind – this is very often the case in real life!

- What you must include in your project, however, is a final design for what has actually been produced, as this is what will be used to assess whether the design work could be implemented by a third person, or whether an efficient and effective design has been produced. You may find that you change just certain parts of the design – in which case just include the new designs for these parts of the solution.
- The important thing is that whatever design work is present be clear and easy for someone else to follow.

TO DO

1 Start your design work with an overall plan – a hierarchy system, a list of what you need to design, something that will help you to follow through and ensure that you include a design for all elements of the solution.

2 Use your inputs, processes and outputs to help you do this.

3 Get your teacher to check your designs.

4 Ask someone else who is familiar with the software that you are using to see whether they could implement the same solution as you from your design work.

5 Keep checking your designs as you implement the solution to make sure that you are doing what you intended.

6 Always go back and check your design work when you have finished implementing the solution – it is easy to forget what you were intending to do when you get involved with solving the problems of building the solution.

Remember the purpose of the design work – it is not a lot of boring, irrelevant pieces of paper. It is included in a project to provide evidence of your skills in this area.

The lack of design work for commercial systems can cost lots of money in the rewriting of solutions or solving of problems – so learn the right way to do it now!

Each of the next chapters deals with design for implementations using different types of generic software package, although there are general hints that you can pick up from all of them.

Spreadsheet software

There are several books available that show you how to use spreadsheet software and include sample designs that you may look at. The examples of design shown here are possible methods you can use – they are not definitive instructions.

Remember that the design work you do must include designs for **all** of the elements of your solution. Processes, for example, may be covered by designs for macros, formulae or user forms.

| Designing a worksheet

Figures 8.1 and 8.2 show design sheets for a worksheet. Look carefully at these to see the amount of detail shown on them. Notice that it is possible to read and clearly see **exactly** what is needed.

Many designs seen in projects are so untidy that no one else can follow them, and do not pay sufficient attention to detail for 'third party implementation' to be possible.

This design has been produced by printing off a blank worksheet and filling it in by hand. It is also possible to use the software to produce the design, but sometimes this can be mistaken for the actual implementation of the solution; so be careful how you present it, and don't just print off what you have implemented.

Figure 8.1 shows the part of the design that gives the general layout in terms of the positioning of items on the worksheet. It also shows items that

	A	B	C	D	E	F	G	H	I	J
1		ROWLANDS EXPENSES CLAIM								
2		EXPENSES SHEET FOR:			A	T		R		
3		DEPARTMENT		W			DATE			
4		STAFF NAME		B						
5		NUMBER		C						
6										
7		DATE	REASON	MILEAGE	BUS/TRAIN	TAXI/PARKING	MEALS	ACCOMMODATION	OTHER	DAILY TOTAL
8		D	E	F	G	H	I	J	K	V
9										
10										
11										
12										
13										
14										
15										
16										
17										
18										
19										
20										
21										
22			TOTAL MILEAGE		L					
23			RATE		M					
24			CLAIMED		N					
25										
26			OTHER		O					
27			TOTAL		U					
28			TOTAL FOR	P			Signed	S		
29		Please attach all receipts								
30										

Figure 8.1 Rowlands expenses claim – constants, variables and layout.

REF	CELLS	NAME	DESCRIPTION	EXAMPLE	FORMAT/SIZE	FORMULA
A	E2	cmonth	month claimed for	May	text up to 9 char	entered by user
B	D4	ename	employee name	Jones	n/a	entered by user
C	D5	enumber	employee number	1234	9999	Lookup D4 in employee table
D	B8:B20	exdates	dates when expenses occurred	25th	dd	Lookup D4 in employee table
E	C8:C20	exreason	reason for expenses	visit to Cadbury factory	text up to 30 char	entered by user
F	D8:D20	exmileage	mileage	102	9999	entered by user
G	E8:E20	exfares	rail and/or bus fares	£27.80	£999.99	entered by user
H	F8:F20	expartax	taxi/parking	£5.34	£999.99	entered by user
I	G8:G20	exmeals	meals cost	£15.45	£999.99	entered by user
J	H8:H20	exaccom	accomodation costs	£125.56	£9,999.99	entered by user
K	I8:I20	exother	other costs	£12.06	£999.99	entered by user
V	J8:J20	exitemtotal	total for day	£186.21	£9,999.99	=sum(G8 to I8) and copy into V9 to V20)
L	E22	totmiles	total miles for month	5,678.0	9,999.9	total of D8 to D20
M	E23	milerate	mileage rate	40.00	£99.99	Lookup from mileage table
N	E24	milecost	cost of mileage for month	£2,271.20	£9,999.99	E22*E23/100
O	E26	excosts	all other costs for month	£12,054.45	£99,999.99	sum J8 to J20
P	D28	exmonth	month of claim	May	text up to 9 char	=E2
Q	E28	exyear	year of claim	2002	9999	=F2
R	H2	cdate	date claim made	6/2/02	dd/mm/yy	=now()
S	H28	exsign	signature of claimant		n/a	entered by user
T	F2	cyear	year claimed for	2002	9999	entered by user
U	E27	extotal	total expenses for month	£15,045	£99,999.99	E24+E26
W	D3	endept	department employee in	Sales	text up to 15 char	Lookup D4 in employee table

Figure 8.2 These design notes give information about the design in Figure 8.1. The letters in the 'REF' column correspond to the bold labels in Figure 8.1. Notice also that cell codes quoted here refer to Figure 8.1.

are **fixed** – those actually written in, as they will appear in the finished solution, for example 'ROWLANDS EXPENSES CLAIM'. The areas/cells that are labelled with letters and/or shaded indicate data that will be entered either by the end user or by the software as the solution is used. Examples of these are **B**, where the member of staff enters their name, and **L**, where there is a formula in the cell.

Spreadsheet design notes

This part of the design (Figure 8.2) shows the detail that is needed to allow a third party to implement the design **exactly**. You could include some of this as annotated comments on the first design sheet (Figure 8.1), but if you have anything at all complicated there may be too much to read clearly. Using a table allows the design to be kept clear and structured, which makes it easier for someone else to read.

Notice what is included:

- references to the layout design sheet
- the exact cells the reference refers to
- names for cells or areas of the worksheet to be used for referencing in formulae
- what the cells actually contain, e.g. a customer's name; the names used can be abbreviations – often means they are shorter so easier to use in formulae
- examples of the data that will go in the cell – this determines the cell formatting and can be used as test data
- the format needed – this indicates the width of columns, decimal places, currency, percentage formats, etc.
- where the cell contents come from – entered by the user or produced by a formula

Even with this level of detail, there is still information missing that would be needed for exact third party implementation.

Examples of other things that might be included are:

- how the worksheet is to be used in the solution
- this may include reference to printing:
  - number of copies
  - headers and footers
  - landscape or portrait
- reference to saving:
  - how saved, macro or shortcut, not automated
  - naming of worksheet saved
  - frequency of saving
- the font style and size
- any special features, e.g. italics, bold, coloured text and backgrounds
- how the solution is to look to the end user (although this may be dealt with as a separate design common throughout the solution):
  - gridlines
  - scroll bars
  - row and column headings
  - toolbars
  - display of zero values

Below is an example of this additional information, for the template design above.

Additional notes

The template will be used for employees to enter their own expenses at the end of the month.

They are to print off two copies, one for their own use and one to submit to Accounts.

Each month's claim is to be saved on a separate sheet using the employee number followed by two digits for the month and two for the year, e.g. 12340502.

Text formatting

Body text: font style Arial, size 12 point. Row 29 to be italicised.

Heading: font style Arial, size 14 point, bold.

Area B7 to J20 to have solid cell borders in black.

Cells E2, F2, D4, H28 background shaded yellow.

Header: 'Employee expense sheet' in Arial 14 point, bold, right justified.

Footer: date of printing, left justified.

On screen, no row or column headings or grid lines should be shown. Any zero values should be displayed as blank. For the hard-copy report no row or column headings or grid lines should be shown. Any zero values should be displayed as blank. Cut-sheet A4 is required, with landscape orientation.

Other elements of design in spreadsheet solutions

Macro design

One other common element that has to be designed for spreadsheet solutions is macros. This is where you combine a set of instructions together so that they are activated by a keystroke combination or by pressing a button to which the macro is assigned.

You can see below a sample design. Notice the key elements of this:

- It is not written in code – this makes it easy for anyone to write. You don't need to know Visual Basic to write a macro design as it simply lists what you want it to do.
- It includes the name to be given to the macro – this avoids you having to make them up as you record them when implementing your solution, and usually means you end up with a project that is easier to follow as you can use this name throughout.
- It shows how the macro is started and where it ends. A macro is a simple program. When you start it off you pass control to the software until it ends – so it is important that you think about where you want the user to be when it does end.

Sample Macro design

Name: Printandsave

Shortcut: Alt Ctrl P

Started from: invoice template

Started by: either pressing button marked 'Save and Print' on template sheet or by using shortcut keys

Actions:

1 Selects area A1 to J30

2 Sets print area

3 Sets print layout to 100%, landscape

4 Sets header and footer – see requirements page xx

5 Sets to print 2 copies

6 Prints 2 copies

7 Renames sheet from new invoice to combination of date and invoice number – ddmmyy9999

8 Saves sheet to folder containing unpaid invoices under sheet name.xls

9 Deletes sheet

10 Returns user to introductory sheet and leaves cursor in cell A3

Ended: when cursor in cell A3 of introductory sheet

There are other things that you might want to design, for example if you are using user forms, but from the examples you have seen you should be able to create your own, including that all-important detail for **third party implementation** to be possible!

Relational database management software

If you don't do design work for this type of project before you start to implement the solution you will get stuck! It is absolutely essential that you make your design efficient and capable of doing what the end user wants. So what does this mean you need to do?

As for any solution you will have data that needs to be input, processes that have to occur and outputs that are produced.

The data

In database projects the first thing is to design the data structures needed. The proper name for the technique used is **normalisation**, and is used more in A2 projects. (This is discussed at greater length in *ICT Coursework for A2*, and many other textbooks.) At AS level the organisation of the data can be done by a process of observation and common sense! What you are trying to achieve is efficient and effective data storage and retrieval. In plain words this means being able to store the minimum amount of data, organised in a way that makes it easy to find everything you want when you want it!

It is worth reading up about normalisation and trying to understand what **entities** (something that you keep data about) and **relationships** are. (Relationships are simply how entities are connected.)

You must avoid:

- duplication of data
- storing data that can be calculated e.g. ages, totals

- storing data that is inaccurate, i.e. has been input incorrectly

You must make sure that:

- data is stored with relationships that allow you to get to every piece of data you need to create the outputs required
- if any data records are deleted all dependent records are removed

You will be expected to include an 'entity relationship diagram' as part of your design, and the designs for all data stores, including any validation on fields and input masks to prevent invalid data being entered, must be shown.

Precisely what you need to design will depend on the software that you are using, but the essential elements of any relational database management software solution to a task are:

- the entities (things) and what data is to be stored about them
- the relationships between the entities (things)
- the way in which data is to be input
- the processes involved in transforming data into information
- the way in which information is to be output – on screen or as hard copy

In one common RBDMS terminology we are looking at:

- tables
- forms
- reports
- queries
- macros
- relationships

Making it easier for yourself – reducing the amount of work needed!

One problem that students have when producing database solutions is that there seems to be an awful lot of very boring repetitive design work to do. Students always seem to end up with lots of queries and input or output forms to design, as well as menus and reports.

It is worth remembering some of the principles of good interface design, i.e. that interfaces should be consistent and familiar for users. In other words, why not have a common design for all input forms, whether they be for customer, supplier or order details? Why not have a common way of producing a design for a process?

With a common design for a menu, for example, you might consider:

- the size of the form and elements in it
  - headings and subheadings
  - buttons
  - logo
  - text labels on or beside buttons
- colours and fonts
  - of text
  - of backgrounds
  - of headings or buttons
- positioning
  - how big should the heading box be?
  - how far from the left should the buttons be aligned?
- What options will be common on all forms?
  - exit?
  - return to main menu?
  - add?
  - delete?
  - amend?
  - reports option?
  - help?

Common Interface design for Forms

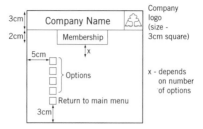

Figure 9.1 Initial sketch for a common design.

If you do one hand-drawn design which shows all of the above, then all you need after that is a table or similar, showing what is different on each individual form. So if you had ten menu screens you would end up with one hand-drawn design that is basically the same for all of the menus, and one table showing what is different on each one!

Figure 9.1 shows a rough initial sketch that would need to be improved to go in a project, but gives some ideas for what a common design should include.

If you have read through the previous section on spreadsheets you will have a better idea of the sort of detail that is needed in design to enable **third party implementation** which is what you are aiming for. Could someone else pick up your design work and produce **exactly** the same solution?

It is possible to design your solution based on **processes** and you may decide that this is the approach to take. The example below shows a sample design for a process.

A possible rough sample process design

Add a new member to the database

This process can be started by selecting the option **add new member** from the **main menu** screen (switchboard).

Require:

> **Button** (b_add_member) on **main menu** to activate:
>
> **Macro** (M_add_member) to open input form
>
> **Form** (F_add_member) for data to be entered through from source document (possibly a membership application form)
>
> **Table** (**members**) on which the form is based and where data will be added
>
> **Button** (b_return_to_main) on input form to activate:
>
> **Macro** (m_ return_to_main) to take user back to main menu

This is a simple example, but there are lots of things you could include if you wanted to make it more complicated. I have included it to show you one possible approach. Here are some of the advantages of doing it this way:

- You find out what you need before you start.
- You have to work out how to do things – so check your software knowledge before you get too involved.
- You get a better idea of time needed to implement the project.
- Implementation and testing can be better organised.
- Testing can be based on testing a whole process, so doesn't end up as a list of button-pressing tests!
- You should find designing the individual things that you need easy.
- You should find designing your test strategy and plan easier.
- Your documentation should be clearer.

There are different methods of designing a database solution and your teacher is likely to have preferred ways of setting the design out, so take their advice.

Just remember that it doesn't make you cleverer if you think you can produce the solution first and then do all of the design afterwards. Many professionals have tried this and suffered the consequences – long hours and late nights trying to sort out problems at a late stage of implementation, or end users who say it isn't what they want. Any student who does not include good designs will limit the mark that they can achieve.

Word processing, desktop publishing and other software

Word processing/desktop publishing software

As mentioned earlier in the design section, it is useful to have a checklist of all of the items needed to produce your solution. An example for a desktop publishing solution to producing a leaflet for a hotel conference centre, to be sent to conference organisers wishing to book the centre, is shown below.

Items needed for conference centre leaflet:

1 hotel logo
2 location information to include:
   a) national map
   b) local map showing station, motorways, main roads and greater detail near hotel
   c) written directions from:
      i)   north
      ii) south
      iii) railway station
   d) distance from airport
3 address
4 telephone, email and fax number
5 conference centre manager name
6 details of room sizes and layouts available and cost of each (possibly in a table)
7 details of car parking facilities
8 advertisements for room deals and delegate rates

9   security statement

10 facilities available for delegates

Once you know what is wanted you can proceed to designing alternative solutions to suit your end user. This can consist of a series of hand-drawn alternatives showing possible layouts and positioning of different items. You should include the **fixed data** actually written on to the designs, with text/picture boxes indicated for where **variable data** would be added.

Figure 10.1 shows one sample rough design for a leaflet to be produced as A4, folded once. The two sides of the leaflet are shown separately. If you do some rough drafts to show your end user, make the leaflet up and fold it

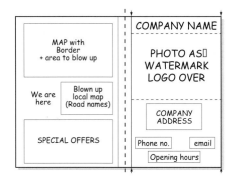

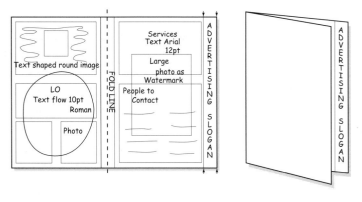

Figure 10.1 Sample rough design for a leaflet.

exactly as the finished product would look. This one would be single-sheet A4 folded off centre.

You will have determined things like fonts and folds and borders in the specification, so designs are purely for layout.

Use of software

Remember that you probably have a far better idea than your end user of what desktop publishing or word processing can produce, and you may need to actually show them a few effects that can be achieved using the software. Examples of this would be watermarking with scanned-in photographs and the alteration of pictures and maps.

Do not use designs that are provided as templates as part of the software. These will show little evidence of your skills. They are designed for the novice user who has little in the way of ICT skills. You are expected to show detailed knowledge of the software.

In most projects it is quite acceptable to use other software to manipulate images or text, for example drawing software or a photo editor, as well as scanning software. You will almost certainly end up doing this with any desktop publishing project.

The end user

The greater the input from the end user at this stage the better, and the more evidence of their involvement that you can include the better. What you don't want is to give the impression that you have just decided for yourself what is required. Copies of sample designs with comments from the end user written on, rather than lists of requirements with ticks and initials, provide good evidence. If they don't like the position of an item on a page then get them to write this on, or show where they want it. With a desktop publishing/word processing product first reactions are very important.

You should produce several alternative designs – the number will depend on how tight your constraints and requirements are. Generally you will then get the end user to select the final design and implement only that one, but you may find that you need to implement more than one design before you get a final product that the end user is satisfied with and that meets the performance criteria. End users like to change their minds about what they want.

Selection of the final design may need your end user to consult colleagues or management, and any evidence that this has happened should be included in your report.

Remember this solution should be useable by the end user in the end user's environment. Designs for any customisation of the user interface to make life easier for the user, and for any back up or security that the user needs, must be included if these are appropriate to your project. Customisation might include items like removing menus or toolbars or options on them, taking off scroll bars, setting the magnification, and so on.

Functionality

Don't forget to consider how the final product will look. It is not suitable to produce a business letter through mail merge that ends up squashed into the top third of a piece of A4! What types of envelope do the company use for sending letters out? Are they window ones, A4 or A5 in size? This will affect your layout.

If the product is a leaflet, is it designed for people to pick up and put in a pocket or bag? Would A5 or a three-way fold be better than A4 for this?

Could you include any items as headers/footers rather than text on the page? Remember that if using word processing software you will need to include features such as conditional mail merges to enable you to use advanced functions of the software. When you have conditional mail merges you will need to consider the layout of letters very carefully.

Accuracy

Designs must be accurate. If you need to leave 2 cm of white space in the

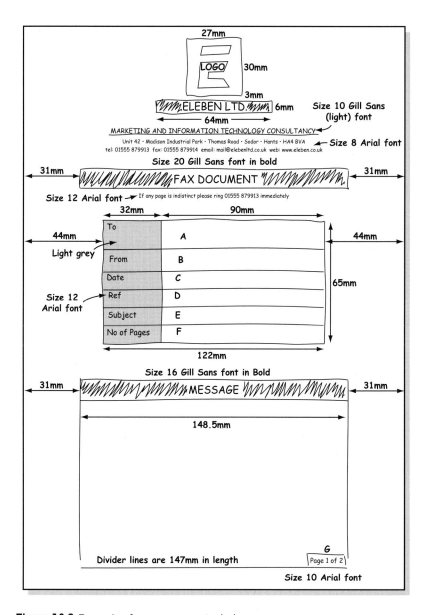

Figure 10.2 Example of a more accurate design.

centre for folding, then this must be shown on the design. If the printer will only print up to 1 cm from the edge of the paper then mark this on. Measurements should be shown accurately.

If the final design is not accurate third party implementation will not be possible. This is one area where many 'presentation', word processing and web projects fail. There is not enough detail shown in the designs for someone else to replicate what the students have done. Figure 10.2 shows an example of a more accurate design.

Processes still matter

As for other projects, don't forget to include designs for processes. For example, how is a mail merge going to work, where will it be activated from, what will it do, what are the inputs to it and the outputs from it? If the product is a newsletter or menu, then how will the end user print it out? How will they amend prices or insert articles?

Web authoring software

Many of the considerations for word processing/desktop publishing projects can be extended to web-based projects. Design needs to include consideration of navigation, layout and structure for the whole site as well as details for each page and the processes involved. The work for each page can be repetitive, so consider having a standard design for all pages/frames and then showing what the different content will be on individual pages.

Many people fail to see what processing is involved in a website project. You must make sure that this is clear in all sections of your project.

Think about the following:

- Size of page and screen sizes: do you want the site visitors to have to scroll up and down, or can you make it easier for them?
- Designs for any icons used, menus, sounds and animation.
- Should people be able to move to any page from any other page, or will there be different types of visitors who will have differing needs? The answers to these questions will have already been found out, but how will your designs take them into account?
- Consider processes. Will visitors to the site be able to enlarge any

pictures? Print items? Send emails? Submit data? These processes need designing.

- If emailing is included, how will this work? How will emails be saved? In a different folder?
- How will the end user be able to update data input to the site? Or load additional pages, remove pages or change pictures?

General authoring software

Similar considerations to websites are involved with any authoring software. You need to be aware from the work that you have done in specifying the problem how the solution is to be used; how the end user (the person who commissions the solution) wishes the people who will work with the software to use it; and what the solution is meant to achieve.

For example: an insurance company wants a solution that will enable new employees to learn about the products that the company sells to customers. They need the employees to be able to gain knowledge from the software, to be able to dip in to different areas when they forget or need some pieces of information reinforcing. The end user is the insurance company, the improvement in employees' knowledge is what the solution is aiming to achieve. Different employees will wish to use the solution in different ways and any design must take this into consideration.

The hardest thing with this type of project is that you need to understand something of the psychology of how people learn and take in information to enable you to provide an effective solution. This could be a suitable area for you if you are studying subjects like psychology as well, or wish to go on to producing educational software – there are lots of opportunities for people who understand these issues.

Presentation software

Some students choose projects based on providing presentations for particular purposes. These have similar requirements to web-based projects and other authoring projects. Again it is important to have some understanding of why and how different functions of the software are used. For example, why use animation? Include sound? How long should delays on slide changing be? What do all of these achieve – are they keeping people interested and alert?

The end user here is the person who wants the presentation producing. It could be a school department wanting something for an open evening, or a teacher or trainer wanting a presentation that students can use for research on a particular topic or which shows them how to conduct an experiment. It could be a company who want a presentation on a new product to take around the country, or a business consultant wanting to explain how to manage a project to a group of employees. The uses of presentation software are endless.

Again processes must be considered:

- How is a slide to be inserted or deleted?
- How can data on slides be changed?
- How will slides be linked to, say, spreadsheets?
- How is the presentation to be started?
- How does the user flip from slide to slide?
- Can they move backwards or forwards?
- Do they need to know how to change the presentation for different audiences? Or to change the font for different sizes of room?

Summary for all types of solution: important points to remember

To produce an effective solution that is useable by the end user in the end user's environment, it is essential that, for all but the most technical end users, the solution be easy to use. Don't expect your end user to be adding data in the datasheet level directly into the data source using a relational database management system. Don't expect them to be able to type directly into a text frame in desktop publishing projects. Make it easy for them!

You will probably find that the solution that you produce will change as you develop it from the initial design. This does not matter; it shows that you are learning more about the software, or about the user's problems, or that the user has changed their mind – this is very often the case in real life!

What you must include in your project is a final design for what has actually been produced, as this is what will be used to assess whether the design work could be implemented by a third person, or whether an efficient and effective design has been produced. You may find that you change just certain parts of the design – in which case just include the new designs for these parts of the solution.

The important thing is that whatever design work is present be clear and easy for someone else to follow.

TO DO

1   Start your design work with an overall plan – a hierarchy system, a list of what you need to design, something that will help you to follow through and ensure that you include a design for all elements of the solution.
2   Use your inputs, processes and outputs to help you do this.
3   Get your teacher to check your designs.
4   Ask someone else who is familiar with the software that you are using to see whether they could implement the same solution as you from your design work.
5   Keep checking your designs as you implement the solution to make sure that you are doing what you intended.
6   Always go back and check your design work when you have finished implementing the solution – it is easy to forget what you were intending to do when you get involved with solving problems of building the solution.

Remember the purpose of the design work – it is not a lot of boring irrelevant pieces of paper. It is included in a project to provide evidence of your skills in this area.

The lack of design work for commercial systems can cost lots of money in the rewriting of solutions or solving of problems – so learn the right way to do it now!

11

Designing testing

Too often testing is something that gets left until the last minute. It is very important that you do not do this, as testing takes time, and without a good test strategy and plan you will lose marks on the testing section as well as in the specification. Without proof of what the solution does then the evaluation marks will suffer as well! To put it bluntly, a poor project is one that does not include good planning for testing.

You need to be able to understand the significance of testing and be able to see the logic of designing testing before you have implemented the solution.

In some project work you are expected to show evidence of corrective action as well as successful outcomes – in other words you need to include evidence of some of the tests that you have carried out that don't work. Students do not seem to like doing this, but it shows that you have recognised when things aren't working and put it right. This is an important skill in ICT. Very rarely will something work first time, and even if it does you need to check that it will always work, no matter what you throw at it!

The aim of testing

Too often candidates assume that the aim of testing is to 'find any bugs' in their solution. This approach is to be discouraged! Testing is to ensure that your solution performs as stated in the performance criteria, meets the requirements of the end user and can be used by them in their environment.

Put simply: **the solution should do what it is supposed to do!**

In order to test your solution well you need to have clear performance criteria and end user requirements. You also need to be organised and methodical in your approach. In the testing section, you will need to prove that you have carried out the tests that you planned.

Before you start to design your testing you will need to know and understand three things:

- what it is that your solution is supposed to do
- what the reasons for testing are
- what types of test you can use

Types of testing

Your teacher will probably cover different types of testing with you and give you some practice at designing different types of test for different situations, and for use with solutions created in different software packages.

In ICT the use of a 'modular' approach to testing is to be encouraged. Because solutions are usually made up of lots of separate parts, calculations, searches, combining pictures and text and so on, it is important to test one part before you try testing all of the parts together. If you don't do this and something doesn't work then it is much harder to tell where the problem is. Modular testing is just like checking all the different parts of a new car engine are working before seeing whether the car starts!

There are four different types of test that can be used.

Unit testing

As the name suggests, unit tests deal with one particular element of a solution. They could be tests on the validation of an item of data being input or on the use of one function. Examples might be tests on cell/field validation, quality/effectiveness of a scanned item, an IF formula on a spreadsheet or a calculated field on a report.

Integration testing

Here more than one element is tested at once to investigate whether links, data transfers and so on work, or whether certain elements combine to give the correct visual effect. Lookups in spreadsheets or macros, queries in database projects, layering of items in desktop publishing, mail merges in word processing projects, links between frames on websites, combining sound and visual effects in a presentation – all of these are examples of where an integration test could be used.

Integration tests are also used to test individual processes within a solution. So for example you might test adding a new customer, finding the price of an item, producing a letter, sending an email, or updating match results.

This type of test expands the purely mechanical test of 'does this button work?', which should always be avoided. Now you can test whether the button takes you to the correct form to enter data or allows a new record to be added.

System testing

When you have made sure that each of the individual elements works, and data can be input, processed and output correctly, you need to take a set of data right through the whole solution. If, for example, you were producing a solution to provide and record invoices for a builder, then you might have to start by inputting the relevant data, looking up prices, calculating totals, printing and saving the invoice and adding the invoice details to a list of new invoices. A system test would take you through every route within your solution in the same way as an end user would want to use it, with real (or realistic) data.

If possible you should have prepared your solution in such a way that you can now test whether it will work in the end user's environment – for example with a stand-alone rather than a networked PC, saving/accessing data from a particular file setup, or using a different version of the software. This is not always possible for you to achieve in advance and will often be part of the end user testing.

End user testing

End users are often very bad at knowing what you want them to do to test a software solution. If you were asked to test a new pair of training shoes you would have some ideas, but you probably wouldn't think about seeing how they washed or what happened if you ran 50 kilometres continuously in them. Computer end users are the same unless they themselves are used to producing and testing software solutions **in a logical and rigorous way**.

It is often a good idea to suggest the testing that you want the end user to do. You might give them a pre-prepared sheet of instructions and questions to complete. An example of part of one of these is shown below. If you do do this, you need to go back to the end user's requirements and make sure that the testing you get them to do will prove whether your solution meets their requirements, or what its problems/limitations are. This will then give you the evidence that you need to include in your evaluation section.

Sample testing questions/tasks for the end user

Here are some examples of questions that you could ask your end user. There are examples for different types of solution.

- How clear were the instructions for installing the invoicing solution?
- Did you find the user guide helpful in explaining any error messages that you had?
- Could you add records easily?
- Did you find the customer report easy to produce? Did it meet your requirements?
- Has the task of preparing a menu been speeded up?
- Do customers find the leaflet on the hotel attractive? Have you had any comments?
- Did you experience any problems deleting a pet's details from the database?
- Were your audience kept interested by the presentation?
- Did you find it easy to update the web page showing match reports?
- Have you had any emails as a result of opening the website?

Obviously there are lots more questions that you could ask. Don't just give the user the solution and ask what they think of it – you are unlikely to get anything useful back from them.

Remember that even if you have done a project set by your teacher you need to show the solution works for your end user – this is why it is much easier to actually have a real end user.

Don't pretend that you have had the solution tested by the end user if you haven't, or pretend that your friend is the end user, and don't submit letters that are supposed to be from the end user but that you have written yourself – this is cheating!

If you have more than one end user of your solution, for example a secretary and a manager, then they should both test the solution as they will probably be using different functions of the solution or may have different skill levels.

Do not forget that the user guide must be prepared before the end user tests the solution, and their testing should include testing the user guide itself.

There are three elements to the design of testing:

- the test strategy
- the test plan
- the test data

See the next chapter for more on these.

Test strategies, plans and data

Good test strategies, plans and data will meet these criteria:

> 'An appropriate test strategy has been determined. An effective and full testing plan has been devised. The testing plan includes the test data, expected outcomes and directly relates to the requirements specification'.

Test strategies

This is where you outline the approach that you intend to take to test your solution. You should describe what is to be tested, in what order, using what type of test. The test strategy is usually not too detailed, but sets the framework for the rest of the testing work.

The test strategy shows evidence to a marker that you understand the process of testing, the types of test available and the idea of 'modular testing', and appreciate the idea that you are testing as the solution is being developed.

Test strategies will differ from one solution to another in order to relate directly to the requirements specification. For example:

- In a database solution you will need to enter data into the data stores before you can test any queries. This will probably mean that you combine entering the data with testing validation rules. You need to test the queries before you base reports or forms on the results.
- In spreadsheet projects you will need to test Lookup formulae and if statements before you can test totals, VAT calculations and so on.

- In desktop publishing projects you might need to test margins and printer settings before incorporating other elements into a leaflet.
- In website projects you will need to test individual pages before you link them together, and launch your site before you test viewing it using different browsers.

Sorting out your test strategy can save you a lot of work. Imagine that you are creating a database solution. You are going to have to enter data into your data stores at some point. Don't enter it and only later think about testing the validation. Test the validation when you first enter the data. You only need to be organised and remember to keep the evidence of the validation tests for your testing section.

In all projects there is a logical sequence of testing. You will need to perform **unit tests** before **integration tests**, and **system tests** after all other testing, but before **end user testing** – you don't want to give the end user something that you know probably won't work!

Note

It is impossible to test every possible combination of actions that can be taken, or every possible combination of data that may be input. If you have 40 different data input fields, each with a validation check on, could you possibly find time to test them all and what would this actually show about your testing skills? It is important to be realistic; much better to show a range of different tests than pages and pages of the same sort. The test strategy allows you to describe how you will show a selection of validation tests on particular data items, and that you would then include similar testing on all validations, or on every web page or frame, or on every slide in a presentation.

Be realistic and think about what you are trying to prove to a marker. Testing takes a lot of time.

In summary, a test strategy sets out how you are going to go about your testing – it is the overview.

Test plans

These contain the detailed descriptions of every test that you intend to carry out. You may decide that the best way to organise your plan is to divide it into sections based on the different types of test you will carry out, or on the different elements of the solution. You may want to show all tests to do with input, output and processes separately. It really doesn't matter so long as the test plan is clear and easy to follow, and allows you to test that the solution does what it is supposed to do.

There are some things that all test plans should include. These are:

- A number for each test.
- What is to be tested.
- Why is it to be tested – what are you trying to prove?
  - You might relate the test back to the performance criteria or end user requirements.
- What data is to be used to perform the test?
  - This might be an individual value or a set of test data.
- What you expect to happen using the given test data.
  - This will include whether error messages will be displayed.

If you have set performance criteria for your solution, then designing tests should be a lot easier. You may even find that you decide to change the wording of your performance criteria to make them easier to test. Here is an example of what this might mean.

A student sets the criterion that 'The solution should work to 100% accuracy'. This would involve a large number of tests. It would have been better to make a more precise criterion – such as that 'all values displayed on an invoice should be 100% accurate' or 'the total stock value should be calculated to the nearest £'.

You will find it easy to make general criteria, but a lot harder to test them!

Remember too that the test plan is supposed to relate to the requirements specification. This is one way you can ensure that it does.

Many students find it easiest to use a table or tables to show their test plan; your teacher should be able to show you examples from past projects. The following table includes examples of different types of test for different projects, to give you an idea of the sort of thing to write.

Sample test plan

Test no.	What	Why	Test data	Expected rest
1	Validation on age field in student table	Ensure validation works and only ages between 16 and 19 accepted	1(a) 12 1(b) 16 1(b) 19 1(d) 24 1(e) xx 1(f) 17	1(a) Error message 25 displayed: user not allowed to continue until data corrected 1(f) Data accepted: user can proceed to take enrolment
2	Process 2.1: add a new customer	Ensure new customer details can be added to the customer table	See data set 3	Customer table contains a new row containing the input data
3	Time taken to enter new customer details	Ensure system meets criterion 1	Test data set 2	Time taken should be under 2 mins from calling up form to returning to main menu
4	Saving macro	Make sure an invoice is saved to the '2002 invoices' folder	Test data set 1 entered into invoice before macro called and invoice saved as Brent01	Brent01.xls should be listed in the '2002 invoices' folder

Test no.	What	Why	Test data	Expected rest
5	Output: mail merged letter	Check layout of letter looks professional with different lengths of names and addresses	(a) short name and long address (b) long name and long address (c) long name and short address (d) short name and short address	End user considers letter to be appropriate for a professional office to send out to customers
6	Process: finding description and price of item from product code	Ensure the correct description and price are looked up when the product code is entered	Enter code 121 in product code and 6 in quantity	Description contains '5 cm nails, galvanised'. Price per item should be 30p
7	Menu choices	Consistency across website	Move to each of the six main areas of site, returning to the home page after each	The same menu should be displayed with the current area highlighted in red

Description of tests in table

There are several points to note on the simplified table.

- For test **1** there is a range of data. It is entirely up to you whether you number each individual validation test separately, or use this sort of approach. **But** you must test using a range of data. This is an

example of a unit test.
- The range of data in test 1 includes **valid within range**, **extremes**, **invalid out of range** and **erroneous** data (that is, if the validation has been set to accept numeric values only between 16 and 19!).
- Test 2 shows how numbering processes can help with testing design. This would be an integration test, probably involving the testing of a button, macro, form/sub-form and a query.
- Notice that in test 2 the data is quoted as 'data set 3'. Data to be used for integration, system and end user tests can be specified separately – usually easier than trying to fit it into the table.
- Test 3 shows how it is important to design the testing to ensure that the performance criteria set are tested. Don't ever specify 'fast', but *how* fast – and then you can test it!
- Test 4 is an example of testing an element of the solution: checking that the saving macro actually saves the required data with the right name in the right place. This is very important when making sure that the solution will work in the end user's environment.
- Test 5 is testing an end user requirement for professional-looking letters to be produced. This is a qualitative test that needs to be carried out by the end user themselves, as their opinion may differ from yours.
- Test 6 shows an example of testing a process. Here data has to be entered which is then used for two lookups to find the corresponding details in a table. This is an integration test.
- Test 7 could be used to test the criteria that 'the visitor to a website should always know where they are on the site' and 'they should be able to move to any area from the home page'.

If you produce the test plan as a separate spreadsheet or table in a word processing package then you can print it out to include in a design section, and then print it again with two more columns added for:

- the actual result
- the location of the evidence of testing itself

These can then be included with the evidence of the tests having been performed. This is sometimes easier to do if you divide the test plan into sections, and show the first section of the plan followed by all the test results for that section, then the second section of the plan, and so on.

Test data

You are expected to use a range of test data. If you look at the sample plan above you can see that in test **1** there are valid and invalid values, values at the extremes of the scale and erroneous or incorrect data. It is expected that normal, extreme and erroneous data will be used in all testing.

It is usually easier to work out what this means for tests where a single data item is tested – the validation rules, for example, or the result of a calculation or simple search.

Other types of test:

- In a desktop publishing project you might test what happens if the user exceeds the recommended number of words for an article in a newsletter/text box.
- In a letter you might test what the layout looks like if you have someone with a very long name that is merged into a field.
- What is the effect of a 10 second delay on a slide presentation?
- What happens to the loading time for a web page if you insert a picture that is 15 megabytes in size or 1 megabyte into the page?

The best source of sample data is the end users themselves. If you have collected documents from or about the organisation they will probably include some test data that you can use; this can be your normal data.

Sometimes you need to have a number of sets of test data to ensure that you have sufficient data to test your system fully. There is no point in having a database that only includes five records when you want to test a report that is multiple pages long and has 10 records on a page, or a query that returns only one value when the normal would be 20 or more.

Normal data used for testing should be realistic. It should not be made up from names of music or film stars, friends (unless this is suitable) or imaginary addresses that show your own particular interests, for example Saruman, The White Tower, Middle Earth!

Equally, in order to avoid problems with privacy and data protection legislation, test data should not include data that is personal and could be related to living human beings. If you are producing a solution for a medical centre then the marker does not want to see real patient details, names, addresses, illnesses, and so on. This would be totally unprofessional and is an important ethical issue for students of ICT and computing.

Single items of test data can be included in your test plan – see test **1** on the sample plan above. Where multiple values are needed it is often best to describe these as sets of test data, such as a set of names and addresses. Make sure that when these appear in your design they are not simply a printout of the contents of a customer data store that you have already implemented, when they are supposed to be sets of data for testing the adding of a new customer!

Plan your testing carefully, but be ready to modify it or to add in extra tests as the solution progresses. Remember you need to collect evidence of the tests that you have carried out, so start doing this from the first day you start your implementation!

Implementation – general guidance

This chapter is intended to help you to decide on the best way in which to present the evidence needed to meet the criteria necessary to get a good mark on implementation.

The criteria from the AQA AS ICT specification are:

1   **An effective solution has been developed that is operable in the proposed environment by the intended end user.**

2   **Appropriate data capture and validation procedures, data organisation methods, output contents and formats and user interface(s) have been used.**

3   **Generic and package specific skills have been fully employed in an effective and appropriate manner.**

4   **The selection of the chosen hardware and software facilities has been fully justified in relation to the solution developed.**

How you actually implement your solution and the software that you use is outside the scope of this book. This is covered by other books, and there are plenty of materials available on how to use all of the different types of software. This chapter aims simply to help you show how you have met the above criteria. Marks are lost by students failing to provide evidence of what they have done, as well as through using only very basic functionality of the software.

The most important thing is that no matter what software you have used or what features of that software, you must be able to prove to the marker what you have done. This section helps you show what you have achieved and how you have achieved it in such a way that it is clear to a marker.

It may sound simple, but it is one of the areas where many students lose marks, often because they just don't think in advance about what they need to do. It is important that evidence is provided specifically to illustrate your implementation. Do not rely on printouts included in the testing section or in the user guide to be the only evidence.

Pitfalls

Most students tend to want to get straight on with implementation, often without bothering to do any other work in analysing the problem or designing a solution. These students think they know what is needed, and will either ignore the end user's needs or think that they know better. They will be disappointed when they find that a query on a database won't work because they have the wrong database structure! There is nothing more frustrating than having spent hours or days implementing something and then finding it doesn't do what is required, however slick the implementation, and having to go back to the start.

Collecting documentation

Many good students fail to get the marks they want because they can't be bothered to do the documentation – they can't see the need for it. 'It works, doesn't it?' is a favourite expression used by this type of student. The student who is prepared to work methodically and provide the necessary documentation will get a better mark than the one who can't be bothered, even when their knowledge of the software may not be so good. This is simply because they are prepared to do the necessary groundwork to achieve their target of a good mark.

Time planning

It is also important to remember that you must achieve a **working** solution. Sometimes this may mean not being able to complete everything that you intended or having to compromise on the way that you do a particular task. Running out of time and having to compromise can be avoided partly by making sure that you choose a suitable task in the first place, and partly by good time planning and organisation.

Implementation evidence must show that the solution does actually work and does what it was supposed to do.

Admitting you don't know how to...

The other key thing that often determines the success of a student in project work is their willingness to ask questions and admit when they are stuck, rather than just giving some excuse for not having done what they were supposed to!

This is one of the most important things to be able to do, as anyone working with computers will tell you. ICT is an area where there are often several ways to achieve the same result, where people work in teams and discuss problems, and where people are not afraid to ask for advice. You may find this hard to do, but it is the way to learn more. No one will think that you are stupid because you don't know how to do something in the software you are using. They may begin to wonder if at the end of three months you haven't got anything to show for your work!

Using your teacher and other students

Teachers like helping students – it's what they are there for, so use them! Also don't be afraid to ask other students how they have managed to do something. So long as you do it for yourself in the end there is nothing wrong with learning techniques and functions of software from other people. You can also use other people outside of school or college to help you, and any books or materials that you find.

The important thing is that you admit that you have done this when you declare what is your own work. If you submit work done by someone else as your own in any project work, it is classed as cheating, and you can be disqualified not only from ICT but other exams as well. It just isn't worth it. Moderators are experienced at looking at project work and can spot when a student doesn't know what they are doing because they have copied the work from someone else!

Thinking you know it all...

This is equally dangerous. It happens when a student thinks that they know all there is to know about the software that they are using, particularly about programming, and that no one can teach them anything! This is a good case of pride before a fall: this type of student fails to appreciate that they need help on how to actually produce a project and document it in such a way as to gain them the maximum mark. It also often means that the solution produced by this type of student is inefficient – they don't always know the best way to use the software. These students often produce projects that include large quantities of rambling code.

How to go about it

Start with an overall plan of what you have got to make. This is what your design work should give you.

If you are doing a database project you should now know exactly what data stores and relationships you need, and what queries, forms, reports, macros, buttons and menus you require.

If your project is a desktop publishing one then you will know the overall size and shape you need, and the margins, fonts, text boxes, graphics, maps, photos and logos that need preparing.

For a spreadsheet you will know what sheets you require, lookup tables, macros, userforms, and so on.

The easiest way to keep track of how you are doing, and manage the work, is to have a list of every item that is needed to make the overall solution. This is part of time planning.

Time planning

Pace yourself

Your project is probably going to be the biggest piece of work that you have attempted so far in your time in education. It is not something that can be achieved over a weekend, or that you can leave until the last minute and rush to produce. It is a piece of work that shows evidence of many skills, and planning and organisation are just two of them.

You may find that your teacher sets deadlines for you to complete certain stages of the project; if they don't, then you need to do this for yourself. It is also important that you try to stick to these deadlines. The temptation is often to leave producing any documentation until the end and just get on with creating the solution. Projects where students have done this do not tend to make the high grades.

It is also worth remembering what was said in the first chapter about the importance of achieving a good mark on the project work, as it has a big impact on the overall grade that students achieve. You can't just swot up for a project; you have to work at it all the time.

Planning implementation

Time planning and being generally organised is particularly important during the implementation phase of the project, as it is likely that you will spend more time on this than any other section of your project.

It is also likely that you will be working on the implementation not just in lessons, but at home or during spare time at school or college. This means that you have to make sure that you use your lessons sensibly; if you need help with a problem you have all the necessary documentation or disk with you when you see your teacher. There is nothing more frustrating than trying to help someone solve an implementation problem purely by having to visualise it!

Using the 'modular approach' means that you tackle the problem in stages or bite-sized chunks. Take a database needing processes to add, amend, delete and query customers, orders and suppliers. It may be more sensible to implement each process just for customers first, then move on to orders and suppliers, rather than doing a bit of each simultaneously. This is because you will be showing new skills with each process, but they will be the same skills for adding a customer and adding a supplier.

Some projects may require less time for implementation than others. This can depend on how much time you have spent on design work and how well you know the software before you start on your project. Obviously the better you know the software the more you will know about available functions, but it is how well you understand the problem that you are trying to solve that will have the biggest impact on your success, so don't skimp on the specification work!

Some examination boards actually require evidence of planning to be shown as part of the project report. There are several ways of doing this. Gantt charts are frequently used, to show, for example, the need to have testing going on at the same time as implementation. The important thing is that you show a realisation of the need for planning, that implementation has to be carried out as a sequence of steps, some of which must occur before others. You can't implement reports based on queries if the queries don't exist; you can't layer objects if they aren't there to be layered!

Naming things

Whatever type of project you are doing, you are going to create objects and files that will need to be given names. Think about this in advance and develop a simple clear naming convention that you can use.

For example you might call everything to do with customers 'cust', for example cust-input-form, cust-table, cust-new-report.

On a leaflet you might have lftmenu, lftmap, lftlogo, lftadvert and so on.

The main thing is that the names have some logic that allows you to identify what they are and makes it easier for someone else to read.

Names such as query1 and query2, newreport and so on are vague, and you will have difficulty remembering what they mean.

If you have an overall list then decide on the names in advance before you create the objects. Also find out whether you can use underscores or other symbols in names.

Keeping your work safe

If you haven't already, set up a separate folder for all of the work to do with your project. This will make it easier to back up your work and transfer it from home to school and to the end user.

Be careful about saving work in the correct version if this is an issue that is important with your project.

Your school is likely to take regular back ups, but do you back up your work at home? It is your responsibility to look after your own work, and you can't recreate a project of this size easily! Back up procedures will be covered in the theory modules; working out your own will help you to understand the issues involved for companies. Questions such as whether you need to back up daily or weekly will be important.

You should create a word processing document into which you can put screenshots when you need to take them, and can write simply about what they show and the date they were taken. This helps when you come to write up your project, and can form the basis of your project log.

Corrective action

It is important that you record not only your successes but the things that fail as well. If you scanned in an image and it is too faint, or you used too dark a colour for a watermark and can't see the writing on top, then include these and then show how you have improved them. If a letter prints out with the wrong layout, the margins aren't correct or the date is not entered automatically, then include the sample and show how you improved it.

Types of evidence

This is just a rough guide to what to include for some types of project. Obviously the evidence that you can provide from different pieces of software is different, and every project will be different.

The important thing is to realise what the evidence is there to show. It should also include only what is actually needed – more printouts does not necessarily mean more marks!

Annotation

Most printouts and screenshots contribute very little to proving what you have done if you don't prove that you understand what they show about your knowledge, understanding and skills. They are also not much use if you don't tell the marker what they are printouts/screenshots of.

Including a title and description, making the printouts a readable size and annotating them are essential parts of this proof.

Annotation can be incorporated into a word processed document, or it can be hand written. You can use different coloured pens to write it in. You can use highlighter pens to emphasise key elements: things that you want the marker to specifically notice. Think about ensuring that they get noticed, to prove what you have done!

Using 'pre-written code', templates and/or wizards

Many pieces of software on sale to the general public contain features that are meant to make life easier for the purchaser. These include wizards to help create commonly needed items such as invitations, invoices, orders, letters, reports, buttons, forms, and so on. There are also templates available for many of these in a library that is purchased along with the software. Using these is meant to be easy; they are designed for non-specialist users who do not need to understand how the software works in any but the most basic way.

If you are a computing or ICT student then you are expected to be able to do more than simply use these. You are expected to have a greater knowledge and understanding of the software that lets you use it to a much greater depth than a member of the general public.

This is why there is an emphasis on using advanced features of the software. You can use wizards, but you are then expected to be able to understand what has been produced as a result, and be able to change defaults set by the wizards. You may be able to record a macro, but for good marks you must be able to understand the code produced, amend it to fit your exact needs and write other pieces of code that can't be recorded.

If you generate a form using a wizard then you should be able to go into the design view and again make changes and customise the end result so that it fits your end user's requirements.

- An inexperienced user will look at what is available, and change what they want so it fits in with what the software provides in the way of templates, and so on.
- An experienced user will use the underlying software features to produce exactly what is needed; they change the way the software is used to meet their own requirements.

In some projects it may be sensible to use a pre-written piece of code, or set of instructions. Software developers have libraries of such items. An example would be the code for a counter on a website. There is nothing wrong with using anything that is freely available, so long as you do not break copyright law, declare where it has come from and do not try to pass it off as your own work!

Warning

Never try to claim things as your own work when they are not. Most markers and moderators have years of experience of teaching and marking and know all about students trying to do this. They also recognise work taken straight out of textbooks! The only person who will lose out if you fail to declare something will be **you** – it is considered to be cheating.

| Advanced features

One person may not be able to use a particular piece of software as well as someone else. They may use different features from one another. For example, a user of spreadsheet software who works in the accounting section of an organisation may need knowledge of all of the accounting functions available, while someone doing research work may need the statistical functions, and someone creating a word game might need to know more about the features available to customise the user interface. All of these can be advanced features.

Just because you have customised the user interface does not mean that you have correctly used advanced features. At this level it is more about whether you have put underlying theory into practice and ensured that the way you have customised the software meets the end user's needs.

An example of failure to do this is the student who produces a beautiful (to them) multi-layered database solution using bright pink and green for screen colours, but who has failed to recognise that these are inappropriate colours for a piece of software being used continually for 8 hours every day; or has omitted crucial options from menus, such as always being able to quit or return to the main menu from any level.

The examination boards provide guidance on what they require in the way of advanced features to use when using different pieces of software; your teacher should have information on these and you can gain more guidance from textbooks.

Note

Do be careful about using off-the-shelf guides to software packages. Many of these only go into the software to a very limited extent as they are designed for the general public user.

So how much writing is needed?

Some exam specifications require a project log or a commentary. These are basically the same thing. You need to explain to a reader what you have done, in what order, and prove it using the printouts and screenshots you have taken. Short paragraphs with well annotated readable screenshots are easier to take in and give a clearer picture to the marker than pages of continuous prose.

Pages of printouts with no annotation or commentary to hold them together show little about what you have done.

Document this section with evidence of implementing the different parts of your solution in the same order as you created them, so that the reader sees the logic in how you built the solution. This will enable you to highlight places where you needed to take corrective action.

You may find it easier to include some of the testing within the implementation. If you have separated tests into sections and have carried them out as you have gone along, then it makes sense to include them in the log at the point where you carried them out. Another advantage is that this documents the grounds for any corrective action – you tested your initial version and found that it didn't work.

The main problems are:

- keeping this part organised
- remembering to include things that haven't worked
- remembering to take printouts and screenshots as you go along
- being careful not to run out of time
- avoiding writing a detailed account of how to use the software rather than how you created your solution

Some basic points to remember

- The implementation section is all about evidence. You have got to prove you did what you say you have done. An external marker or moderator does not actually see your solution working on a computer system.
- Put your evidence in a logical order and show the progression in the work that you have done.
- Make sure that you take screenshots and printouts at regular intervals during the time you spend implementing your solution.
- Keep evidence in a safe place, and have a back up copy. Examination boards are not very sympathetic to ICT students who lose their work – they should know better!
- Make sure that any printouts or screenshots that you use are readable – remember your eyesight is probably a lot better than the marker's, and a marker who has to get a magnifying glass out is not going to be in a good mood!
- Screenshots and printouts need to show something – don't include lots of them just to make your project look bigger.
- Remember that you might understand what a particular screenshot is showing but a reader may not. You must put titles on all of them.
- Annotation or labelling is essential. This is what you use to point out what you want the reader to see.

- Annotation must be clear and readable. Too much is as bad as too little if it affects the readability.
- The reader does not want to know how to use the software.
- The reader wants to know how you used the features of the software to create your solution – what you have done.
- The reader is looking for proof of your abilities to use the software in the best way that you can.
- It is expected that your use of the software will be more involved than that of an average non-specialist. This is why the use of advanced features needs to be demonstrated.
- Lots of screenshots or printouts simply bundled together prove nothing. It is the writing that goes with them that shows your understanding and how you have developed your solution.
- Generally you will improve your solution as you spend more time working on it. It is important that you show how and where you have made improvements.
- Remember that you are not allowed to submit any work on disk or CD. This is an examination board rule.

Chapter

14 Implementation evidence: spreadsheets

If you are doing a spreadsheet project, for every worksheet that you use you will need three pieces of evidence:

1 a screenshot as the user will see the sheet
2 a screenshot as you see the sheet when you are working on it – the developer's view
3 a printout of the formulae used

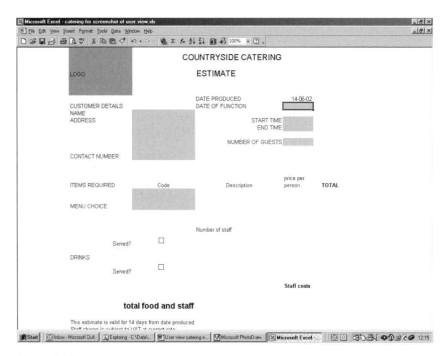

Figure 14.1 Printout of a user's view of a worksheet.

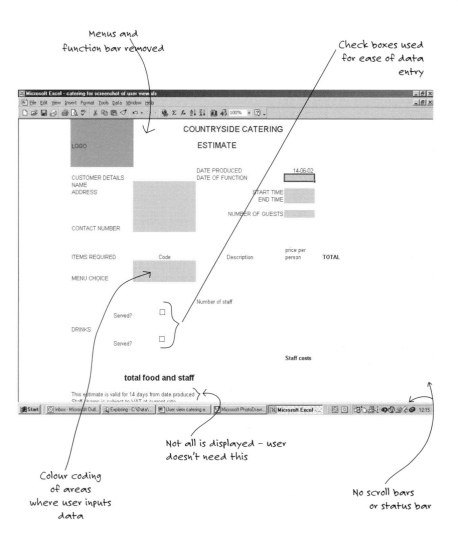

Figure 14.2 Annotation on a printout. The annotation draws the reader's eye to what you want them to see. It also proves you understand what you have done

These are the bare minimum. If you don't include the first one, the marker will not be able to see how you have customised the interface, removed sheet tabs, scroll bars, gridlines, customised menu options, set magnification, and so on.

Estimate sheet – user's view

Figure 14.1 shows a printout of a user's view of a worksheet. Notice how all gridlines, row and column headings, scrollbars, toolbars and so on have been removed. This now shows the screen exactly as the user will see it. You need to include shots like this to show clear indications of where you have customised the interface. But like all screenshots it will provide little evidence of your abilities unless you annotate it to show the main features. Figure 14.2 shows an annotated version of the same view: see how the annotation draws the reader's eye to the features that you highlight.

You may notice too that the layout is not perfect in that it fits exactly on the full screen. Sometimes you have to compromise between the screen view and the printed version. In this case the user will prepare the estimate in the office but the printed version will go to the customer – so the most important item is the printed version.

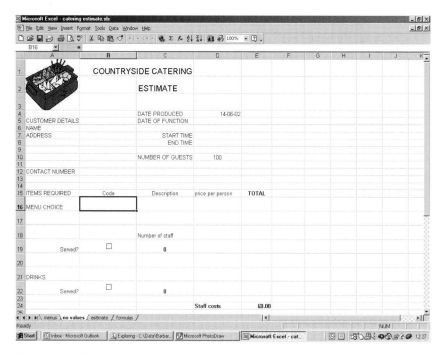

Figure 14.3 Developer's view of the solution in Excel.

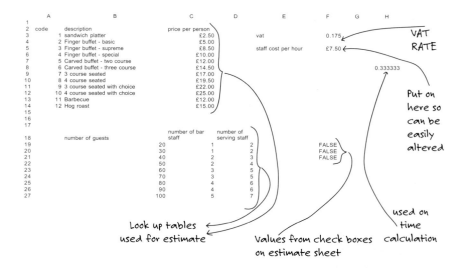

Figure 14.4 Annotated developer's view of worksheet containing look-up tables and calculated fields and constants.

Estimate sheet – developer's view

Figures 14.3 is a developer's view of the solution. This is as you are working on it. This can be used to show individual features such as a validation rule, or comments on cells, or just to give an overall picture of the solution as it develops. It is likely that you will use several of this type of screenshot.

Be careful that you don't cut down shots like this too much so that the reader can't see exactly what is being shown – particularly if it takes longer to do.

Figure 14.4 shows part of the same workbook, but this is a separate worksheet that will not be displayed when the person is using the estimating sheet. By removing the sheet tabs you can prevent them from accessing it. This means that there will be no user's view of this worksheet. It is also why the sheet tabs will be removed on the main sheet, so that the user cannot move to this sheet and alter the tables – this would be the job for the manager and would not be included in the general instructions in a user guide.

Estimate sheet – formula printouts

The formula printouts (see Figure 14.5) are essential to prove that there are formulae there and what you have used. Typing in the figure on screen, putting 'C1+C2+C3+C4', or 'sum (C1:C4)' will all show the same on a screenshot! Therefore the marker needs a formula printout to give credit for using the sum function. Formula printouts must have row and column headings and gridlines, and must have the column widths altered so that all of a formula can be seen on a screenshot. Remember the marker will not be looking at this on screen. For example, if all the marker can see of a formula is:

```
IF(C5<E6,(VLOOKUP(B6
```

. . . they will not be able to see whether the formula is correct and will work. It may be an idea to have two copies of your work, with one set up so that you can print out formulae easily.

Figure 14.6 Printout of estimate.

	A	B	C	D	E
1					
2		ESTIMATE	COUNTRYSIDE CATERING		
3					
4			DATE PRODUCED	=NOW()	
5	CUSTOMER DETAILS		DATE OF FUNCTION		
6	NAME				
7	ADDRESS				
8			START TIME		
9			END TIME		
10			NUMBER OF GUESTS		
11	CONTACT NUMBER				
12					
13					
14					
15	ITEMS REQUIRED	Code	Description	price per person	TOTAL
16	MENU CHOICE		=IF(B16="","",VLOOKUP(B16,menus!A3:C14,2))	=IF(B16="","",VLOOKUP(B16,menus!A3:C14,3))	=IF(D16="","",D16*D10)
17					
18			Number of staff		
19	Served?		=IF(D10="","",IF(menus!F19,(VLOOKUP(formulas!D10,menus!B19:D28,3)),0))		
20					
21	DRINKS				
22	Served?		=IF(D10="","",IF(menus!F20,(VLOOKUP(formulas!D10,menus!B19:D28,2)),0))		
23			=IF(C19="","",C19+C22)		
24				Staff costs	=IF(D10="","",(C23*D9)*staff cost per hour)
25					
26					
27					
28					
29					
30			nd staff =IF(E16="", "" ,(E16+E24))		
31					
32					
33					
34	This estimate is valid fo				
35	Staff charge is subject t				
36	All necessary cutlery, gl				
37					
38	Please contact Country		01875 456777 to confirm the arrangements		
39					
40	Thanking you for your in				

Figure 14.5 Sample formula printout.

Try to use font reduction to fit your formulae on to fewer sheets, while still leaving them readable. Use the print preview function to juggle the size until you fit the formulae on to the minimum number of sheets without sacrificing readability.

Final printed estimate

Figure 14.6 shows the actual printed estimate – as required on cut-sheet A4. This one is blank, as printouts with data entered will be shown later in the testing evidence.

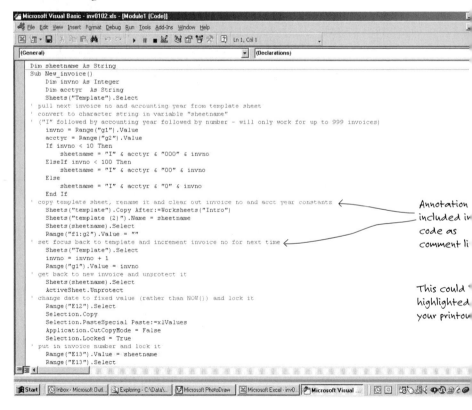

Figure 14.7 Annotated macro code.

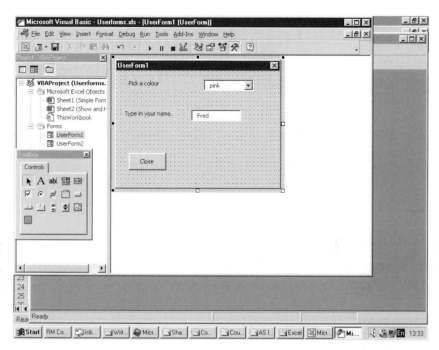

Figure 14.8 A simple user form screenshot – if you use user forms you need to show more detail than this!

In addition to these pieces of evidence you will also need some or all of the following, and will perhaps want to include other things as well:

- macro code – Figure 14.7 shows an example of annotated macro code
- user forms, showing customisation – Figure 14.8 shows a very simple user form; note yours should be more detailed than this!
- menus
- screenshots showing the set-up of folders or shortcuts made for the end user
- error messages

Implementation evidence: database projects

As with spreadsheet projects, there are certain basic requirements for evidence for a database solution:

1 data store designs
2 relationships
3 forms in design view and as the user sees them
4 reports in design view and as the user sees them, on screen and/or printed out
5 queries in design view

Notice the mention of 'design view'. It is the design views that are used to show what you have created. For the data stores this should include evidence of the fields, data types, input masks and validation rules used (see Figure 15.1). You will find that it is not easy to show all of these on one screenshot. So think about how you can prove you have implemented them. Could you include one full screenshot and then cut and paste the other input masks and so on for other fields on to the same sheet to print out?

For reports and forms the same problems occur (see Figures 15.2 and 15.3); but you need to use the printouts to show evidence of changes you have made to default values, calculated fields, links to data stores and so on.

Queries can be evidenced by printing out the grids (see Figure 15.4) or by printouts of the query code, such as the SQL. For example, you can see below some SQL code copied for a query to select students who haven't paid their fees:

```
SELECT students.[student no], students.
[student name], students.fee

FROM students

WHERE (((students.fee)=0))

ORDER BY students.[student no];
```

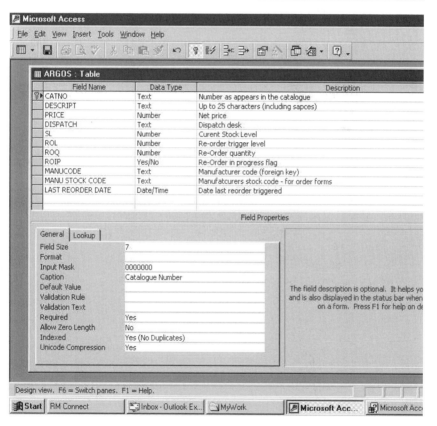

Figure 15.1 This printout only shows the input mask and details for one field. To print these out for every field in every table would be too much. One solution would be to have the details for each field combined on one sheet of paper, or a couple of sheets, by cutting and pasting.

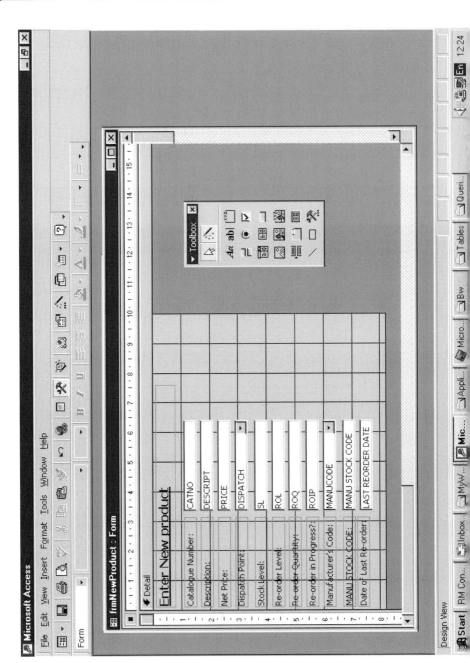

Figure 15.2 A form design printout – no annotation means it shows little evidence
to the marker. Also, where does the detail for each field come from?

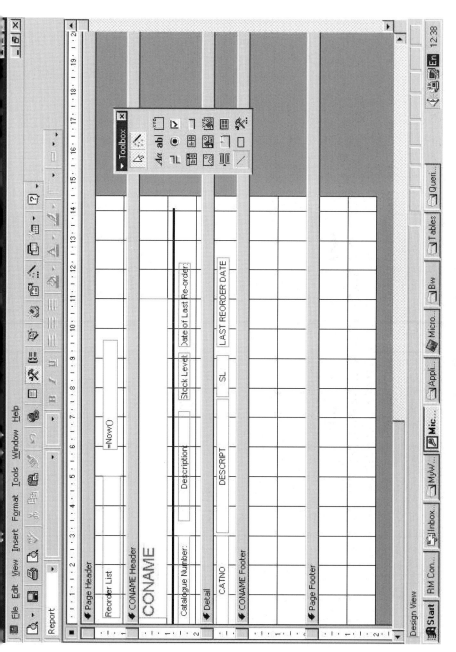

Figure 15.3 Report design view – again, annotation is needed to make the printout into useful evidence.

Figure 15.4 A query screen shot – notice the problem with this is that only part of the query is shown.

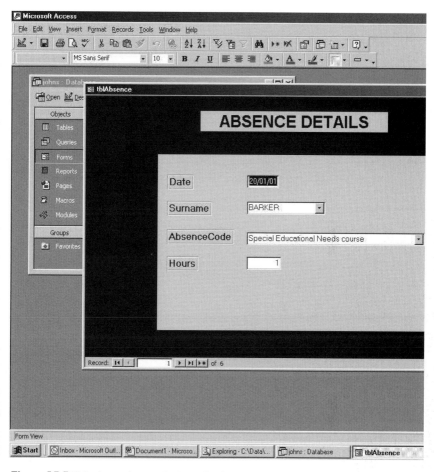

Figure 15.5 This shows the user's view of a form with data selected. Notice the form is not maximised and is not very user friendly.

Again it is important to include screenshots that show how the end user sees the solution. Are windows maximised? Simply printing out a form without showing the actual view to the user does not answer this question. See Figure 15.5.

It is possible to use documenter printouts produced by the software. However, these should be used sparingly, and as with any other printout should not be included without annotation that proves you know what they are showing (in other words, that you understand what you have done)!

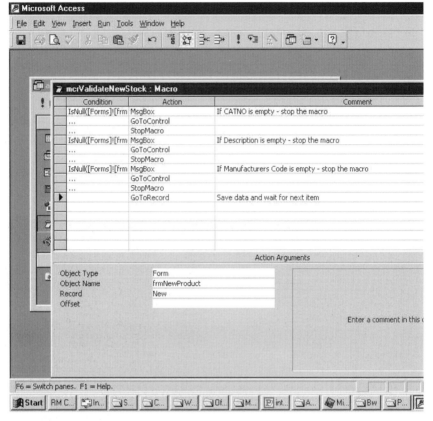

Figure 15.6 Macro written using set commands. No handwritten annotation is shown, although the student would need to show the full conditions. Also, they could add other annotation to highlight any points. They *have* included comments.

There are other items of evidence to include:

- macros (see Figure 15.6)
- modules
- menus
- screenshots to show lists of all forms, queries and reports
- shortcuts and folders used

Figures 15.7 and 15.8 show other examples of evidence that can be included.

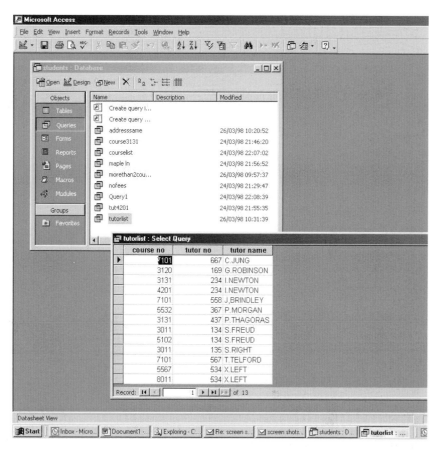

Figure 15.7 Various combinations of views can be used. This one shows a list of queries and the results of running a 'tutorlist' query. Is this a good way of displaying the results of a query? How could you show that it actually works? These would be quesions to consider for testing.

Other projects

As mentioned previously, the evidence of implementation needed will vary with the software used. In presentations it may be necessary to take a screenshot showing how animation or time delays have been set on particular slides, or how an animated graphic has been added to a web page.

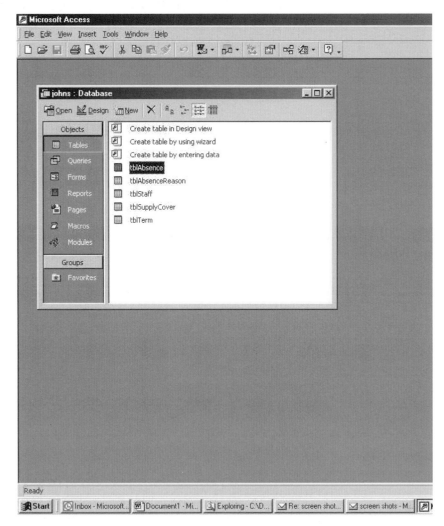

Figure 15.8 A printout like this can be adapted to show a list of implemented features to use as an index for evidence.

However, don't include screenshots of every step needed to create a form with a wizard, or to select a particular function from a menu, or record a macro and assign it to a button!

It is up to you to decide what exactly is needed – with the help of your teacher. The following chapter gives you more guidance on this.

Implementation evidence: word processing, desktop publishing and other software

For all of these types of software, it is important that you can show exactly how you have used the software to manipulate objects, pictures, photographs and text to achieve the final result. In other words, you are trying to show a reader what skills you have and what software features you have used in producing a solution. It is quite normal to use several pieces of software – photo editors, drawing and scanning software often being necessary 'tools' to use.

Elements of the design

In previous sections you will have read about the difference between fixed and variable data – variable data being what you use to test your solution. It is important that you understand the difference between these.

You will also need to produce an overview of the whole solution and a list of items to implement. For a leaflet these might include a template that contains a map, a watermark, images, text and a table. For a website they may be similar, but also include the frames and outline structure for the website, including navigation controls.

It is also a good idea to show the order in which you intend to implement your solution, perhaps by setting up text frames or a standard slide format or by producing a template. Don't be tempted to use standard templates. An ICT student is expected to know more about the workings of the software and about the actual functionality available to them than non-expert users, who rely on standard templates and wizards.

Examples of evidence for individual items

Maps

These are frequently used items. You need to show how the map looked when you scanned it in and the settings used. If it didn't come out clear enough the first time, what did you do to improve the image and what does it look like now? Have you added things to the map? Removed items? Labelled roads or added arrows or a box round it? Show the finished map with annotations to explain what you did and how you have changed the original. The original map is your input data, the finished one is part of your output.

Watermarks and photographic or scanned images

Common problems with these are that you may not get a clear image if you have used scanning software to scan in the image for the watermark. You could use a digital photograph as your starting point and change the intensity of the colours, or change all of the colours to one tone. Show examples of what you have done and why as you improve the watermark and position it.

Photographic images used on web pages can be treated in the same way. Have you had to size the image and perhaps used only part of the original? Have you altered sky colour, added objects or painted bits out?

Avoid using clip art pictures – using these demonstrates little in the way of skills, and little imagination!

Text and tables

Show how these have been set up. Is there any formatting required – type of font, colour, size, orientation? Is the text to be wrapped around an object or superimposed over a picture? Does it flow between text boxes? Have you created text boxes and then linked them through to a file in a word processing package or a table in a spreadsheet package? Sometimes this is a good way of making solutions easier for the user to maintain, for example, when producing newsletters and websites where data needs updating and the end user has no familiarity with the software used to create the solution.

Often you will find that you are incorporating testing of each item as you go along. For example, you could use some text given to you by your user and discover it won't fit into the frame you are using with the font set at a particular size, and have to then change the font size and re-try. Or you might set a time delay for a slide of ten seconds and then discover it changes too quickly, or a photograph may take too long to load on a website.

Sounds

Probably the hardest thing to provide evidence of! You are allowed to submit video evidence and if anything you have implemented includes the use of sound or moving images this is really the only way that you can prove it has been implemented as you describe.

Websites

Do not just include pages of HTML code – you need to show what controls and formatting you have set. Show what frames you have used, links to images, pieces of pre-written code with where they have come from and so on. Printouts of screenshots listing all files involved may be one helpful item to include, as would evidence of uploading the website onto the server. Think about how you can evidence animations and navigation that you have implemented. Think about the list of all files and whether this is something that might be included in your end user guide as well – have you used meaningful names for files that will enable the end user to identify them easily?

Word Projects

Remember not to use pre-produced templates but to show how you have built one up. Don't forget to show layouts that you have implemented for mail merge letters and how these meet end user requirements. When you test these, you must show evidence of all the different possible layouts using different paragraphs and so on in conditional mail merges – your letters must always look professional, not bunched up in the top third of a piece of A4 paper!

Points to remember

It is impossible in a book to show examples of everything that you might want to include in these types of projects so here are some points to remember:

- Save evidence as you go along. Once you have changed a photo or a map you will find it difficult to get a screenshot of the original.
- Annotate everything that you include to show just what it is you have done to it.
- Make sure that every piece of evidence has a title.
- Try to get your end user involved in approving some of the finished items and/or commenting on the different stages, for example 'I can't read the text on top of the watermark clearly, can you change the colour?'
- The writing that you do should help tie the evidence together so that a reader can see clearly the stages that you have gone through to reach the final solution.
- If it doesn't work to begin with then don't leave it out – include examples of the corrective action that you took.
- Do not just include lots of printouts without labels, titles and text to go with them – they will gain few marks.
- Remember to include descriptions of all of the software that you have used and justify its use to produce what you have implemented, for example scanning software, photo editors and so on.

Testing

If you have done a good test strategy and plan already then actually testing your solution should be straightforward. This is what you are trying to prove:

> **'The test strategy and plan previously devised have now been followed in a systematic manner, using typical, erroneous and extreme (boundary) data.'**

Remember that you are trying to prove that what you have produced does what it was supposed to do (end user requirements) in the way it was supposed to work (performance criteria).

You must be honest. Being able to admit that something doesn't work is an important skill, so don't try to only show evidence of testing the bits that work – show the ones that don't and try to explain **why** they don't work.

What the marker needs to see

A marker needs to be able to see evidence that:

- Your solution works.
- It does what it was supposed to do.
- You have corrected any errors that you have found.
- You understand what testing is for.
- You are able to show a range of types of test.
- You have shown evidence of using a range of test data.
- You understand the role of the end user in testing.
- The user guide is tested by the end user.

- You understand the difference between testing in your own development environment and that of the end user.
- You can produce clear, understandable evidence of testing.
- Your testing is appropriate for the software solution you have produced.

What a marker doesn't want to see

- a test plan with the words 'worked' or 'didn't work', or ticks and crosses, and nothing else
- sheets of printouts with no titles
- printouts with no annotation or highlighting or explanation of what they are meant to show
- only simplistic testing of buttons
- only 10 tests (or similar number)
- no evidence of user testing
- 100 pages of tests that show exactly the same skills
- no evidence of planning or organisation to the testing

Avoiding too many printouts

If you have designed your testing carefully then you can have evidence of more than one test shown on a printout. For example, if you are testing the process of adding customer details, then you can have a set of data that includes the different types of data (normal, invalid, etc.). You might have a normal name and address and then an invalid date of birth and telephone number, and so on. Your printouts could then be annotated to show what happens with the different data values.

As with the evidence of implementation, the annotation that you put on your printouts is crucial. You have got to make sure that someone reading your project work can clearly see what each printout shows.

Being able to read the screenshots is important too; do not make them too small so that the reader can't tell what has happened.

Remember that cross-referencing your test evidence to the test plan is important, so make sure that every printout is given a title that relates it to the test numbers in the test plan.

Some examples of sample test printouts complete with annotation are shown here.

Figure 16.1 shows a layout for testing the process of adding data to a database. This is the sort of testing that must be done to show that your solution works. You could do this by having three printouts with annotation. You can avoid the testing of buttons and simple macros by doing it this way – it also saves on paper and time!

Figure 16.2 shows a test printout for an estimating task where the set of test data is given at the bottom – this would normally be included in your testing design but has been included with the estimate for reference. Again this test is designed to show that the solution does work and that the estimate produced meets the end user's requirements. Annotation has been added to highlight items.

Test 26 – Testing adding data to a database

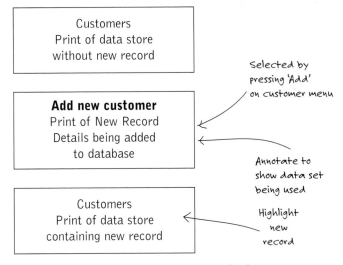

Figure 16.1 Layout for testing the process of adding data to a database.

Test 35 – To test the production and printing of an estimate

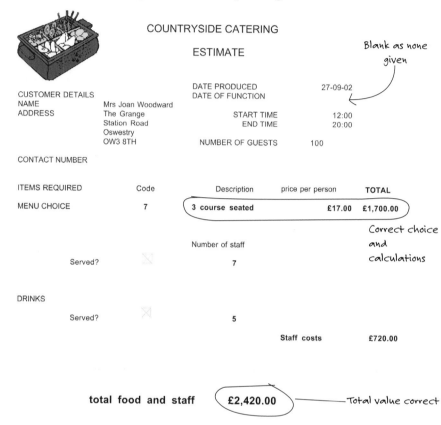

COUNTRYSIDE CATERING

ESTIMATE

Blank as none given

DATE PRODUCED	27-09-02
DATE OF FUNCTION	

CUSTOMER DETAILS
NAME   Mrs Joan Woodward
ADDRESS   The Grange
                        Station Road
                        Oswestry
                        OW3 8TH

START TIME	12:00
END TIME	20:00

NUMBER OF GUESTS   100

CONTACT NUMBER

ITEMS REQUIRED	Code	Description	price per person	TOTAL
MENU CHOICE	7	3 course seated	£17.00	£1,700.00

Correct choice and calculations

Number of staff

Served?   ☒   7

DRINKS

Served?   ☒   5

Staff costs   £720.00

total food and staff   **£2,420.00**   —*Total value correct*

This estimate is valid for 14 days from date produced
Staff charge is subject to VAT at current rate
All necessary cutlery, glasses and crockery provided free.

Please contact Countryside catering on   **01875 456777 to confirm the arrangements**

Thanking you for your interest in our company

Test Data – Mrs Joan Woodward
The Grange
Station Rd, Oswestry OW3 8TH
Christening Party on ?
12 noon until 8 pm
Menu 7, served and drinks service.

Figure 16.2 Test printout for an estimating task.

System Testing: R5

SHOW CALENDAR

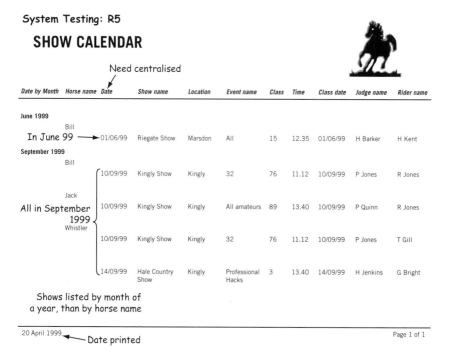

Need centralised

Date by Month	Horse name	Date	Show name	Location	Event name	Class	Time	Class date	Judge name	Rider name
June 1999										
	Bill									
In June 99 ➙		01/06/99	Riegate Show	Marsdon	All	15	12.35	01/06/99	H Barker	H Kent
September 1999										
	Bill									
		10/09/99	Kingly Show	Kingly	32	76	11.12	10/09/99	P Jones	R Jones
	Jack									
All in September 1999		10/09/99	Kingly Show	Kingly	All amateurs	89	13.40	10/09/99	P Quinn	R Jones
	Whistler									
		10/09/99	Kingly Show	Kingly	32	76	11.12	10/09/99	P Jones	T Gill
		14/09/99	Hale Country Show	Kingly	Professional Hacks	3	13.40	14/09/99	H Jenkins	G Bright

Shows listed by month of
a year, than by horse name

20 April 1999 ➙ Date printed

Page 1 of 1

Figure 16.3 Printout of a horse show calendar from a database solution.

Figure 16.3 shows a report output as a result of a query. The end user had asked for a calendar of show dates. Notice that the student has the date and page number on the printout. The fields have been selected to meet the requirements and records have been grouped by month and then by horse. The student has annotated the printout to draw the marker's attention to the relevant areas.

In both Figure 16.2 and Figure 16.3 it is worth noting that attention has been paid to what the hard copy looks like and its readability and suitability for the purpose. Often I see mail merge letters where the whole of the letter takes up about a quarter of the paper − no company would want to be associated with that standard of letter. This sort of thing isn't difficult to do − it just needs you to think about what is actually needed.

Testing as you go along

This is really about saving you time and effort. The more you do as you are implementing your project the less there is to do at the end. Many students leave testing until the last minute and then make a bad job of it, and often do a lot of work for very few marks. Leaving testing until late on is a problem in many ways, especially when there are a limited number of printers and everyone else is trying to finish off their projects!

Make use of any screenshots and printouts you have taken as you have progressed through the implementation.

In some types of project, if not all, you will have done some of the testing as you have been implementing your solution. This will have been explained in the test strategy.

To help you provide evidence of all testing, you might include a copy of the whole test plan again here – this time with the extra columns for:

- the actual result obtained
- any comments on problems
- reference to the evidence that this test was actually done

This enables you to refer back to tests done already during implementation, by quoting page references or similar.

For the tests that have been done during implementation, you can just include the relevant part of the test plan with the implementation section. For example, if you are producing a leaflet using desktop publishing for a conference centre, and one element of the leaflet is a map of the location of the centre, you might have all the tests to do with sizing and readability of the map included when you first implement it. This makes sense as you will be making adjustments to your original map to ensure readability and so on. So do the testing then and save yourself time and effort.

User documentation and user testing

It is important that you complete your user documentation before giving the solution to the end user to test. It is part of the solution produced and so must be tested as part of that solution.

In the chapter on designing testing, suggestions were made for giving your end user tasks to complete and/or questions to answer, so that you get better evidence of end user testing and the end user has a better idea of what they are supposed to be doing.

The completed questions/forms should be included at the end of the testing section, along with any letters or completed questionnaires, copies of emails or any other evidence that you might wish to include to prove that the solution works in the end user's environment and meets the end user's requirements.

Remember that if you have different types of end user, or end users with different skill levels, then they should all test the solution. An example might be a database solution where a secretary adds, amends and deletes records, but the manager queries the database and produces reports.

Do not

- make up evidence – it is easy to spot
- pretend a letter you have included is from the end user when you have produced it yourself
- use your friends to test your system if you don't admit to it
- lie at any point

Why? Because any of these can count as cheating and could lead to examination boards excluding you from gaining an award.

Types of testing evidence

What you can submit as evidence will largely depend on the examination board.

- Submitting work on disk or CD is not allowed.
- Video evidence often is allowed, and may be essential if you have been producing, for example, a presentation for use with an audience. But do avoid a long boring tape that just shows a lot of validation tests; use video evidence only where it is appropriate.
- Screenshots and printouts can provide most evidence of testing carried out by you.
- As mentioned above, letters, emails and completed questionnaires and forms can evidence end user testing.
- Photographic evidence could be of value in some projects – particularly presentation projects.

Testing against qualitative criteria rather than quantitative criteria is not easy, as it relies on you getting people's opinions. An example is where you are trying to improve a company's image and realistically the only way you can measure this is looking at customer comments or sales figures.

This shows up a basic problem with project work – the time scale for testing. It may take six months or more in the real world before you know whether a leaflet is effective in promoting a business. For this examination you are supposed to be able to show it is effective in a very short time.

One student put a pile of leaflets out in a village shop and post office to advertise a local builder, and then watched people picking them up and asked them what they thought of it. She also recorded the number of leaflets taken over a week. This might not be a practical idea for you, but try to think of any method of testing that you can use.

If you have produced a website for a company to improve its image or popularity, have you got any proof that it has or hasn't done this? This one is not easy to do as it takes time to see the result of improved marketing materials, but you could include copies of any emails received commenting on the site. If the website is for a club, could you ask other members to look at it and comment on it?

A presentation could be tested by making a video showing audience reaction, or by giving the audience a questionnaire to complete afterwards. Remember: responses to questionnaires are variable, and only as good as the questions you ask!

Be careful not to spend hours producing all sorts of graphs and other statistical evidence just to prove one point – this will only waste your time.

Problems

The challenge of providing evidence of testing can put a lot of people off using some types of software for projects. Consider how you are going to provide the necessary evidence for testing **before** you start on your project. If you can't come up with an answer on this you will be limiting the mark you can obtain, so rethink your project. It is possible to provide evidence for any type of software; you just have to think carefully about what is needed. If you understand what the solution is actually meant to do then it is easier. For example, what is the website meant to achieve? What should someone be learning from using the PowerPoint presentation?

18 User guides and help

Very often students leave preparing a user guide or adding help files to a solution until the last minute, and end up rushing to prepare something to hand in.

Fairly obviously this is not the way to do it, for several reasons. Firstly, it is a good thing to pick up marks on, particularly if you haven't found other parts of the project easy. It is also a matter of using your common sense and paying attention to detail.

> You will probably know already what makes a good user guide or help section; or at least you know when you are using a bad one! People notice when things aren't easy to use, rather than when they are right. It is a good idea to look at examples of good and bad user guides and to consider what could be done to improve them – and so what makes a successful user guide.

What your user guide will be like depends on the end user, their skills, how much they want to be able to do in future without your help, and the environment they will use the solution in.

Do not forget who the end user is. This is covered in chapters 1 and 2: but it is the person who commissions the solution to use. For websites that is the owner of the shop, the club or the hotel, and not the person visiting the website. For a leaflet it is the business wanting the leaflet, and so on.

User interface and user guides are included in theory work, so anything you do will help you to understand the theory by putting the principles of good design into practice.

Here is a list of things that should be considered when preparing the user guide for your solution:

- **The language used** must reflect the end user. For example, for small children it must be simple, for inexperienced users it should not contain technical terms, and so on. Users do not talk in terms of tables and queries.

- **The use of screenshots** should be considered essential so that the user can relate this directly to what they are seeing as they use the system. It is not only difficult to write a guide without illustrating it, but makes it very hard for the user to know if they are looking at the right thing!

- **Attention to detail** is important. If the user needs to press 'Return' after entering data into a field, then tell them they need to. Similarly, if data needs to be entered in capital letters then examples in the guide should illustrate this. If you've ever tried to search a database that has data stored in capitals only and have entered lower case values, you will know how frustrating this can be. If you have used an on-line data entry form which doesn't tell you whether to use 'tab' or 'Return' to move between fields you will also know how this feels!

- **The actual installation of the system** may or may not need to be described – depending on who the specified end user is. Even if you are installing the solution for the end user they should still know what is needed for it to work effectively, if this is an issue.

- **Start-up procedures** must be included and should be for the intended end user in the intended environment. Procedures should not explain how to start the software on the school/college network system unless this is the end user's environment!

- **The normal working of the system should be covered methodically** – the flow of the guide should follow the way the end user will work with the system. Start by describing how to enter data if this will be the first thing that the user has to do; don't start with printing out reports or similar. In order not to confuse the reader, it may be suitable to just describe normal working and not include error messages until a later section (alternatively you may feel it is better to introduce these where they might occur in the use of the solution).

- **All likely error messages** should be shown and explained. This is particularly important with validation rules. Users also need to know the difference between a cautionary message and one that will not let them proceed unless they change the data they have entered. You should, of course, have made the error messages suitable to your end user's skill level/language so they should know what to do without having to look the message up in the guide, but people do forget – particularly on functions only used occasionally.

- **It should always be made clear to the user what actions they need to take.** Never leave an end user not knowing what to do next – a basic principle of good design, so make sure the user guide follows the principle.

- **Saving data/files** should be included if this is part of the solution. This should describe what to do **in the end user's environment.** Watch out for references to saving on P drive on the college/school network!

- **Back up procedures** must be approached from a similar angle and should be included in most user guides.

- **Security issues and settings** – if these are relevant then they should be included in the guide, including what to do if you forget your password!

- **A glossary of terms** may be included if this is necessary to the user's understanding of the manual. This is like a dictionary at the end of the guide (or the beginning) that explains any technical terms used. In most cases this will not be necessary if the language used in the guide is appropriate.

- **A quick reference guide** may be an appropriate addition for more experienced users. This could take a variety of forms. This could be a simple piece of card that fits in a top pocket or over the function keys, which has reminders of shortcut combinations for macros and other actions. This could also be a more appropriate format where there are many infrequent users of the software who only perform simple tasks.

- **The physical environment** in which the system is to be operated may be important to the type of guide produced. For example, space may be short and a large A4 guide would not be useable in the space available. A small child would need something small and easy to hold, that is perhaps produced on stiff card rather than paper. A user guide used in a kitchen or a factory may need to be coated to prevent it from wearing out too soon in a harsh environment. Also think about how it is to be bound together.

- **The overall structure** of the guide is important. Is an index necessary? Should a list of contents be included? Are page numbers needed?

An increasing number of students like to produce on-line help of various types, instead of or as well as a user guide. Here are some points to consider if you do:

- Don't spend too much time on it. Look at how many marks you can get and adjust your time accordingly. If it means you won't get the testing done or an evaluation completed then it's probably better to stick to an ordinary guide.
- Look at good and bad examples of on-line help. Be critical: what annoys you or what do you find hard to use? Some common criticisms are:
  - 'I can't find what I want without knowing what it's called.'
  - 'The help comes up on top of what I want help about so I still don't know what I did wrong.'
  - 'I can't view the help and the work at the same time.'
  - 'It isn't clear what I need to do.'
- Are resources an issue? Remember sophisticated on-line help is 'resource hungry' and can slow things down.
- Is it actually the best way of doing it? Sometimes the most technically advanced option is not the best. Many people still like to use books. This is perhaps particularly true of older users. Very few of you will have end users who are younger/the same age as yourselves.
- What are you trying to prove? This is the user guide being assessed, not your technical ability.
- Good projects that gain high marks do not need to have on-line help; it is not an essential part of the project.

- If you have produced on-line help it will need testing and you will need to show the contents and how it works very clearly, with clear, easy-to-read screenshots.

It may well be better to settle for a straightforward user guide and pay more attention and time to ensuring that you have followed good user interface design principles throughout your project. Think about adding on-line help if you have the time.

Evidence

Make sure you include a copy of the user guide or help in the exact form in which it would be given to the end user.

Make sure that the user guide won't get separated from the rest of your project, and that it is clearly labelled and has a title, so that if it does get separated it can be put back with the project. (Best to make sure it doesn't get lost in the first place.) Even if it is a different size to A4, consider binding it in with the rest of the project or making an envelope into which to put it in on an A4 page.

Remember, a good user guide:

- covers all relevant aspects including
  - normal operation
  - common problems
- is appropriate to the needs of the end user

19

Evaluation

The evaluation of your solution is probably one of the most important parts of the project, and yet it is often one which is very badly attempted by students. Many students leave the evaluation until they have so little time to complete it that it ends up being a token half page. Others don't even bother to include it at all!

For a good mark on this section the evaluation must prove that

> 'The effectiveness of the solution in meeting the detailed requirements speci-
> fication has been fully assessed, with the candidate showing full awareness of
> the criteria for a successful information technology solution. The limitations
> of the solution have been clearly identified.'

If you have done all of the things suggested in earlier chapters then evaluating the success or otherwise of the solution that you have produced will be easy.

The most important factors that have a knock-on effect on the evaluation are whether or not you have got good end user requirements and clear performance criteria and whether you have carefully planned and carried out your testing.

It is important to remember that you are **not** evaluating:

- how well you know or knew the software you are using
- how well you dealt with the work in the time available
- how much help you have been given!
- whether you feel you have learnt anything from doing the project work

What you are evaluating is whether or not the solution that you have produced meets the performance criteria that you set and whether it meets the end user's requirements.

Not all projects will be totally successful. The constraints of project work and assessment mean that you are not working in an ideal way. As a result problems will occur and you may not have time to solve them all.

Markers understand this and they are looking for your ability to be critical of your own work as well as being able to see where it is successful. The ability to see faults in your own work is essential for success in the world of ICT. Admitting that your solution doesn't work quite the way you or the end user hoped it would is a sign of maturity, and will not lose you marks.

A well written evaluation will:

- show evidence of an understanding of the criteria a successful ICT solution should meet
- take each performance criteria in turn and say whether the solution does or does not meet it
- consider each of the end user's requirements stated in the specification in turn, and evaluate the success of the solution in meeting them
- quote evidence from the testing (and end user's comments and testing) to support statements made
- include any limitations that the solution has – things that may not work as planned or have not been completed
- include any improvements that should be made to the solution to meet the performance criteria and/or end user's requirements
- be an honest evaluation of the success or otherwise of the solution!

Don't ever pretend that something works when it doesn't – a marker or moderator can spot this very easily. They have a lot of experience of assessing students' work and know the tricks that students get up to!

It often shows a greater understanding by the student of their work if they can spot where and why a solution is not successful.

Below you can see some examples of how to write up a good evaluation.

End user requirement:

'The solution should produce a quotation that is 100% accurate.'

This evaluation criterion has been met, at least as far as can be seen from the testing carried out in the time available. When the solution was tested with data sets A and B, the calculations necessary to produce a quotation were checked by using a calculator (see tests 34 and 35). When Mr Green tried out the solution by producing a quotation for a real job, he compared the result he got with his old manual method and said 'This is going to stop me from making a lot of mistakes, I'd forgotten to add in the transport costs when I did it manually.' (See copy of letter from Mr Green on page 97.)

End user requirement:

'The web pages should be easy to navigate for all visitors to the site.'

This criterion was met, as a consistent user interface has been developed for the website. As can be seen on the printouts of web pages on pages 46 to 54, there is a common navigation bar which is always situated in the same place on the page and which has the page that the visitor is currently on highlighted in a different colour. The background page colour corresponds to the colour of the page tab on the navigation bar.

Evidence that this does make navigating the site easier for visitors is shown by the copies of emails received from visitors to the site on pages 67 to 69. The first two emails are from first-time visitors, while the others are from people who have visited the site several times. It can also be seen from their comments that they have visited the site for different reasons and so have needed to navigate to different areas.

End user requirement:

'Stock levels should be adjusted after every order is produced to keep them accurate.'

The solution does not meet this criterion. I had not realised that when people make orders they can sometimes decide part way through that they don't want to continue with the order. This can be because the company doesn't have all of the products they want in stock or the price of an item isn't acceptable. It can even happen at the end of recording an order when the customer finds out he can't get a discount! This problem only appeared when my end user was trying the solution out in his office. He checked the stock levels after he had had one of these cancelled orders and realised the solution didn't work properly. His comments are shown on page 87.

Limitation:

In my solution when an item is added to an order the number of that item in stock is automatically decreased by the number ordered. This means that if the order is then cancelled the stock level will still have been adjusted and will be inaccurate – there will appear to be less stock than there actually is.

Improvements:

To prevent the problem caused by orders being cancelled part way through, I could have a temporary table that stores each order item, and then only adjust the stock levels when the order is confirmed. That way if the customer changes their mind I can just remove the contents of the temporary table and the stock levels will still be accurate.

Final reminders for AS projects

Here are some final reminders on how to submit your project work.

This is a quick check list for you to follow, to make sure that what you hand in is easy to mark – if it is, then the marker will be able to find the evidence more easily to be able to award you the marks that you deserve!

1   Keep to deadlines set by your teachers. These are usually planned so that they can give you feedback and allow you to improve your work.

2   Use techniques to cut down on the amount of printouts and paperwork that you need to include – follow the tips in this book.

3   Make sure that you have a copy of the marking criteria used to assess your project work. There may be other guidance notes from the specification that you can use. Specifications are published on exam board websites.

4   Check that you have met all of the criteria to the best of your ability in the time available.

5   Don't leave anything out that might be useful.

6   Bind your project well so that pages don't fall out. Some exam boards will not let you use hard-backed folders, and you certainly shouldn't use plastic wallets for each individual sheet.

7   Do make sure that your user guide is securely fastened into the project report.

8   Spiral binding with a piece of card at the front and back is probably the best way to bind the project.

9   Make sure the project is labelled with your name, candidate number, centre number, unit entered for and a title.

10 Have a list of contents and use page numbers.

11 Avoid the use of appendices. If something is relevant put it where it is needed – this applies, for example, to designs, sample documents and printouts.

12 Use a spellchecker and a grammar checker, or get someone else to read the project and check it for errors.

13 Listen to comments your teacher makes, and act on them.

14 Don't leave pencil comments by your teacher on your work.

15 Make sure that someone can read your printouts without a magnifying glass!

16 Admit to any help or materials that you have used.

17 Don't think that you can finish a project in a weekend and get a good mark.

18 Remember that marks gained on projects count towards your overall grade. Sometimes one mark on a project is worth two in an exam – in other words poor project work means a poor overall grade.

19 You have control over the project work; you don't write the exam questions.

20 Remember – project work in ICT is more like the real world than probably most other work that you will be doing! So this is an opportunity to get used to it – and enjoy yourself at the same time.